Embracing
Anxiety

Endorsements

"*Embracing Anxiety* is a must-read for anyone navigating the ever-changing and often confounding world of modern work, especially for those of us helping others navigate it as Agile Coaches and corporate change agents. In these pages, you will meet An Bakkes, someone who I have come to know and treasure. Her remarkable story will captivate and inform you. Better than that, what she did as a result of her story will set you up with the insights and practical tools you need to help people work with their anxiety. Make no mistake, Agile provokes anxiety, especially when one didn't get to choose the change. I believe this anxiety, and the many unproductive behaviours that result, are the main reasons that Agile transformations 'fail'. In this book, you will learn a straightforward, yet profound, way for helping people work through the Embracing Anxiety process to become powerful actors in their own lives and in their work."

Lyssa Adkins, Co-Founder Agile Coaching Institute and author Coaching Agile Teams

"The relevance and need addressed by *Embracing Anxiety* is evident in the world around us. In almost every speech, article, news broadcast and conversation the message is one of unpredictability and extreme change at a very fast pace resulting in a disruptive and often incomprehensible world. This means that the experience and familiar pathways we could previously rely on are simply not as relevant. This uncertainty, although exciting, is a sure source of anxiety in our personal lives and in almost every workplace at all levels."

"I admire the honesty and openness of the personal 'journey' that forms the basis of the book and fully appreciate the academic rigour to ensure the value of the model going forward. This book will be very relevant and useful to anyone wanting to develop a more positive and powerful mechanism for coping with and thriving in this world of unprecedented and unpredictable change."

Aletha Ling, Retired Executive, previously SVP Operations, Emerging Markets Digital, Visa Cape Town

"*Embracing Anxiety* is an absolute must-read for everyone, particularly for women in leadership roles. With change being the constant we face in our complex societal roles, the tools and models provided by An Bakkes in this book challenge us to look at ourselves realistically, develop self-trust, love and gratitude for what is, and grow through every challenge we face. By sharing her personal journey, An has provided a solution to a subject that has been a hindrance and sometimes a dead end to many. It is the realisation that anxiety can work for our good that will allow us to face it with resilience rather than struggle with it in seclusion. The book has been a tremendously amazing tool in my personal healing process and has provided me with a brand-new outlook on life."

Keneilwe Mogasoa, Transformation Catalyst, Star Performance Group SA

"I have been fortunate enough to participate in a workshop delivered by An Bakkes that introduced me to her 'Embracing Anxiety' Model. I was both moved by the personal experiences that An so generously shared and that underpin the development of her model and then captured by the process that she had developed. An's book, *Embracing*

Anxiety: Coming back with hope is a tribute to her inner strength, spirit and innovation. Her model captures so elegantly the process by means of which we can embrace this very human experience, develop resilience and grow. Working in the field that I do, school-based mental health, I consider her book a particularly rich resource for teachers and school leaders. These often unsung heroes carry the expectations of many and work in environments that can be extremely stressful. *Embracing Anxiety: Coming back with hope* is a book that offers its readers the opportunity to understand and embrace that most human of emotions – anxiety."

Fiona Pienaar, Director of Clinical Services,
UK Children's Mental Health Charity – Place2Be

"An's personal and inspiring life story sets the backdrop for the valuable insights shared in this must-read book. This is further complemented by her extensive work experience producing relevant reading material which we can all undoubtedly benefit from. This book is not just some theoretical construct – it provides practical and useful tips along the journey of Embracing Anxiety. These insights provide the mechanism to rob Anxiety and Fear of their power and allow each of us to take control of our own lives and circumstances. Failure is often an internally created perception rather than an externally fulfilled reality. Thanks to An for this inspiring piece of literature that can really make for a much richer life!"

Regan Adams – CEO, BNP Paribas Personal Finance South Africa

"In the world of today, where we experience increased complexity and uncertainty in our personal and professional lives, learning to embrace anxiety is crucial for us. An Bakkes' book deals with this subject with insight and pragmatism. An shares her personal journey of confronting and learning to embrace anxiety as a platform for the coaching model which she developed and researched. She explains the concept of anxiety practically and unpacks her model clearly, giving the reader many tools and reflective exercises for purposefully developing their own capacity to live with anxiety. This is essential reading for learning to thrive in these turbulent times."

Kathy Bennett, PhD, Leadership Coach, Part-time faculty
for University of Stellenbosch Business School

"To learn from the wisdom and insight of somebody who has made sense of chaotic and disruptive life events, is truly a privilege. Not only does An allow us an honest insight into her journey but she also abundantly shares how she found factors such as trust, vulnerability, gratitude, acceptance and hope to provide meaningful ways in dealing with anxiety and despair. Her insights, not only made a difference in managing her own anxiety but will keep on making a difference to those around her and to you the reader."

Dr Jopie de Beer, CEO: JvR Africa Group, Managing Director: JvR Psychometrics

"I was really moved by your story, and the way you've not only picked yourself up – but also found it in your heart to offer a map, and with it hope, to so many others who find themselves in similar dark places. You have my respect and admiration for the work that you're doing."

Dr Michael Mol, Medical Doctor, Executive Television Producer,
Presenter, International Speaker and Business Consultant

First published in 2017

ISBN: 978-1-86922-658-9
eISBN: 978-1-86922-659-6 (PDF eBook)

Published by KR Publishing
P O Box 3954
Randburg
2125
Republic of South Africa

Tel: (011) 706-6009
Fax: (011) 706-1127
E-mail: orders@knowres.co.za
Website: www.kr.co.za

Printed and bound: HartWood Digital Printing, 243 Alexandra Avenue, Halfway House, Midrand
Typesetting, layout and design: Cia Joubert, cia@knowres.co.za
Cover design: Marlene de Villiers, marlene@knowres.co.za
Editing & proofreading: Valda Strauss, valda@global.co.za
Project management: Cia Joubert, cia@knowres.co.za
Index created with TExtract / www.Texyz.com

Embracing
Anxiety

Coming back with Hope

by

AN BAKKES

kr
publishing

2017

Dedication

To my husband Tiaan

To my family, my friends, my clients and people who have shared this journey with me in any way. Thank you for the love, support and contribution you make to my life every day. I thank you with deep gratitude.

Table of contents

About the author ii

About the feather.. iii

1. Introduction: My story 1

2. Let's look at anxiety.. 11
    2.1. What is anxiety?... 11
    2.2. What are the major causes of our anxiety? 15
    2.3. Resilience: Coming back with hope...................................... 21
    2.4. Growth vs change.. 27

3. The model.. 37
    3.1. The four pillars... 40
    3.2. The five steps 40

4. The four pillars of the model.. 43
    4.1. Suspended judgement 43
    4.2. Observation 52
    4.3. Love.. 59
    4.4. Gratitude 68

5. The 5 Steps of Embracing Anxiety 81

    As adults, how do we learn a new skill in life? 81

    5.1. Give it a name – identifying anxiety 86
    5.2. The belief systems that inform out fear........................... 91
    5.3. The emotions, mind and body relating to fear................... 97
    5.4. Our fear-driven behaviour 108
    5.5. How to change my behaviour: 5-step summary 118

    Wrapping up 126

References 127

Endnotes 131

Index...132

About the Author

An Bakkes holds a BCom in Sports Management, BA(Hons) in Psychology and an MPhil in Management Coaching. She practises as a Life, Business and Agile Coach. She is a pilgrim of life who spends her time engaging with her passions. These include coaching, interactive workshops, facilitation and conversations that shape people, organisations and the world. An's journey in the world of work includes executive and senior management roles as well as managing mergers and acquisitions. She brings versatility and insight that stretch across disciplines, knowledge domains and different industries.

About the Feather

The feather on the cover of the book represents my personal and professional "logo". It is my reminder and affirmation to live a life that focuses on matters that I perceive as being of lasting importance in this world. The story that informed this turning point began on my 25th birthday.

On this day my father passed away in front of my mom and me due to a massive heart attack. It was in the days after this that I made two lasting decisions in my life. One was to "never become complacent" and the other was to live the best possible life every day.

During the months that followed I came across an Egyptian myth that supported my promise to myself in the most fitting way.

The Egyptian view of the afterlife has two strong views. Upon physical death your soul can go to the following: a place called the "Field of Reeds", where the soul continues to exist in peace and love without death. The other alternative is that the soul simply ceases to exist, implying no afterlife of any kind.

A light version of the myth is as follows: Upon death the soul goes through a process the Egyptians call the "Hall of truth". In order to gain passage to the afterlife the soul goes through a truth-measuring process. The measurement is not based on purity but on how heavy the heart is when compared to a feather. The heart would be placed on a golden scale and balanced against a white feather of truth. If the soul turned out to be lighter than a feather it would be freely admitted to the "Field of Reeds". If heavier than the feather the soul would be thrown on the floor and devoured, as a result of which the soul would cease to exist. A light heart is characterised by love, gratitude, non-judgement, truth, hope. A heavy heart would be full of ego, anger, non-forgiveness and self-judgement. (Please know that this perspective is derived through my filters and I am not citing any research for this other than my interpretation.)

This myth symbolises what I hope to achieve every day. To live my life the best way I know how, until I know more. Some days I am more skilful than others, yet this is how I try to live without taking myself too seriously. As I grow and learn I have also come to realise that our souls might even feel dead or numb while our bodies are alive due to our fear, anxiety, anger and lack of self-love.

So the feather reminds me to try on a daily basis as a coach, mother, wife, sister, friend and woman to focus on connection, people and matters of lasting importance and not on matters of the ego. I must mention that this is Work In Progress and that I do not have it waxed.

CHAPTER 1

Introduction – My story

"I believe it will have become evident why, for me, adjectives such as happy, contented, blissful, enjoyable, do not seem quite appropriate to any general description of this process I have called the good life, even though the person in this process would experience each one of these at the appropriate times. But adjectives which seem more generally fitting are adjectives such as enriching, exciting, rewarding, challenging, and meaningful. This process of the good life is not, I am convinced, a life for the faint-fainthearted. It involves the stretching and growing of becoming more and more of one's potentialities. It involves the courage to be. It means launching oneself fully into the stream of life. Yet the deeply exciting thing about human beings is that when the individual is inwardly free, he chooses as the good life this process of becoming."[1]

This book came to life due to intense personal trauma followed by academic research in the form of a Master's degree and rubber stamped by the workshops and coaching sessions that have since been done using the "Embracing Anxiety Model". The "Embracing Anxiety Model" is part of my process of becoming. In the next chapters I hope to share with you an ongoing journey that requires commitment to self, the willingness to become comfortable with life's discomfort and the courage to choose from a healthy space with every decision that needs to be made.

My life has been characterised by being driven, the need to perform, the need to be perfect and the need to be accepted by all who crossed my path. As you can well imagine, these are all catalysts for an anxiety-filled life on all levels and in all facets. Admitting this ignites far less judgement in me than it did in the past, yet there is still a tinge of self-judgement that rears its head when I read these words. These drivers and needs contributed to my desire to succeed (which included "getting it right" all the time) at everything that I did as well as being accepted in the process of succeeding. It is important to state early in this journey that there is no judgement on being driven. It is about what feeds the drive. Is it fear (of not being good enough, not being successful enough etc.) or is the drive fuelled by the need to grow and be the best we can be from a loving and grateful space? (I am getting ahead of myself.) This was an exhausting way of living to say the least because my decisions where mostly informed by some fear or the other and I was never without anxiety. I walked with this burden every day of my life and I judged myself every moment for feeling anxious. What made it even heavier to carry was that I come across very confident, reasonably well-balanced and very in control of my life. Yet it was because that was how I thought I should be. Today you will see very similar traits in me but it is because of who I am and who I choose to be from a self-aware and loving space. One of the themes in the book is how the outward manifestation of something sometimes looks just the same, but the place where we choose from is where the true power lies.

With all that said, here is the start of my story …

In April 2008 I fell pregnant against all odds with a projected due date of 3 February 2009 and my husband and I were elated. Although we were not obsessed with having children, it was a deep desire and according to the various doctors we had a less than 3% possibility of having children. Needless to say this little miracle changed our way of thinking with regard to the medical world and the potential that resides within the choices we make as human beings.

In September 2008 I was diagnosed with cancer. During this time I was 21 weeks pregnant with our son Luca. I had a malignant melanoma and had Clark level IV and Breslow 3.5 diagnoses. This means that I had the most advanced level of this type of cancer and that the mole was already 3.5 mm deep. (Malignant moles are normally removed at 1mm.) The prognosis was not great. The oncologist and other specialists guessed that I would live for more or less another six months if I did not terminate the pregnancy and start with aggressive treatment.

This was one of the moments when I became aware of dealing with intense complexity on my journey. After crying through the tsunami of emotions that overwhelmed me, I had to tell my husband. I had to tell my husband that I was sick, that I might not make it, and that we had to make a decision around our unborn baby's life. It was at this point in the journey that the wave of uncertainty crashed over me. The doctors, although kind, were clear, clinical and open about what needed to be decided.

The available options on the table were less than exciting and were as follows:

- Terminate the pregnancy (a term that the medical fraternity uses) in order to receive chemotherapy to increase the chances of my survival.
- Keep our baby with the high probability that I would not survive and my husband would have to raise an infant on his own.

The terms "complexity" and "uncertainty" gained new meaning during this time in our lives and during the tough conversations that followed between ourselves, the doctors, our families and friends – conversations that neither my husband nor I were practised in.

Sometimes I think it was due to the fact that we did not fully understand the impact of the prognoses and the situation we found ourselves in, that we made the courageous decisions that we did. Now, with more awareness, I know we both made soul decisions at the time.

We decided to keep our miracle baby and to see how much of the cancer could be removed surgically in order to avoid chemotherapy. Reflecting back to those days, I remember that the intensity of the fear and anxiety was almost unbearable.

I had four operations to remove the cancer and create skin grafts, and numerous tests to try and establish if the cancer had spread and by how much. On 12 November 2008 I was rushed to hospital. There were complications with my pregnancy and on 14 November 2008, at 27 weeks and five days to term, my son Luca was born via an emergency Caesarean. He weighed 1 000 grams. Just for context, a full-term pregnancy is 40 weeks and the average baby weighs between 2.9 kg and 3.9 kg. Luca was born three months too soon,

Luca was in neo-natal ICU for nine weeks and it was during this time that I learned the meaning of true resilience. Luca's first meal was 1 ml of expressed breast milk every hour. He was not completely developed yet. His nails, eyebrows, lashes and nipples where not completely formed, his skin was vaguely transparent and the veins where visible under the paper-thin skin. Despite the support from the open-incubator, the ventilator that helped him breathe and all the pipes, the only way my baby would survive was by gaining weight and growing. Our journey in resilience continued. Luca would gain 10 grams per day for three days and then have a dirty nappy and lose 25 grams!!! And then we would start the process again.

There were times that he needed a blood transfusion due to infection. And a 20 ml blood transfusion would save his life. There were continuous setbacks and the decisions were complex. My husband and I had to make them over and over again without knowing what the future would hold and if our son would survive. This combination of the continuous uncertainty and decisions that had to be repeatedly taken in a complex medical and emotional environment, gave birth to the model that today is known as the "Embracing Anxiety Model".

I was afraid, anxious and terrified all the time. So if I was going to be afraid and anxious every day, I needed to find a way to be in the world that resembled some form of normality. In order to gain some form of perceived control, I started designing a model to deal with and understand my fear, anxiety and overwhelming emotions. Most of all I wanted to use my fear to enable me to survive through this time to the best of my ability. If I was going to be stressed, anxious and afraid for a large part of this journey, I decided that I might as well use it to my advantage.

The cancer was removed surgically and Luca did not contract cancer through the placenta as the doctors feared. We received inordinate amounts of grace.

During that same period I had to go back to work in order for us to remain financially stable. Although this was additional pressure, I found that I could use work as a place to hide from all the fear. It was at work that I started recognising the fear in others. At the time I was managing a business acquisition in the medical health industry and it came as a complete surprise to find that the fear that was inside me also lived in the people at work in different intensities and was manifested in various forms of behaviour that ranged from aggressive bullying to passive resentfulness in the serving of others.

It was during this time that I started coaching people using the Embracing Anxiety Model to understand if others would find value in it. The results of the coaching conversations where amazing. The people who formed part of the conversations grew in their level of self-awareness and started changing in front of my eyes. Based on the process we went through and their willingness, their decision-making processes started transforming to show a higher level of awareness and quality of decision making.

In 2010 I commenced my M.Phil (Masters in Philosophy) in Management Coaching in order to put the model through some robust academic research and practice in a measured environment in order to prove to myself that what I had designed in my hours of desperation, fear and survival could be used to enable other people to embrace their dark hours and use it to their benefit. My wish was that whatever I had learnt could be packaged in such a way that people did not have to go through dark hours to learn and apply some of the lessons and discoveries I had made. Moreover this work could be used in any setting from NGOs to corporates to schools.

It was during the same year that I fell pregnant with Emma, our daughter. Both surprise and deep fear found itself inside me. The joy of being able to have another child against all odds without trying and the intense fear of contracting cancer and giving birth to another premature baby played war inside me and the emotional and medical complexity and uncertainty started all over again.

Due to the pregnancy there were very few comprehensive cancer tests I could undergo. The uncertainty and the fear while holding a corporate position taught me resilience of a nature that I did not comprehend until a few years later. I was termed a high-risk pregnancy, had a little boy of 20 months, worked in the corporate environment and had to perform as a programme manager while I was anxious and afraid every single waking moment.

Every day that Emma was in the womb was a gift. Every day past the 27-week mark was one day extra that she would be stronger and healthier. Emma was born at 32 weeks and weighed 2.0 kg. What a delight. What gratitude we had that our little girl was stable even though premature. It was during this time that I started realising the true meaning of gratitude and what healing and empowering energy it brought. I started understanding that love had a far deeper, tangible meaning than I could ever comprehend. By this time my husband and I had been in survival mode for two years and loving one another started meaning something completely different from when we got married.

We went through a similar process with Emma, the emotional roller coaster of gaining weight, losing weight, infections and this time there was a two-year-old brother at home who needed love and attention and could not understand why his mother and father spent so much time at the hospital where he was not allowed to go. Emma spent six weeks in ICU.

When Emma was three months old I was diagnosed with melanoma metastasis level IV cancer. This means that the cancer had spread to the lymph glands and there was the risk of it spreading to the lungs and brain. I decided to put my studies on hold for a year, something that this type-A personality would never even have considered earlier in my life.

The medical solution was aggressive surgery and a neck dissection was performed. This entailed the neck muscle being teased out between the nerves that allow for feeling and movement in the face, neck and the shoulder. The neck muscle and a part of the shoulder muscle were removed in order to remove all the lymph glands that serve as the first line of defence, yet also allow the cancer cells to spread.

Again a different level of growing took place. At this time I had an infant that I could not hold or feed for three weeks due to the surgery. I realised yet again how much of my confidence as a person, a mother and a wife I took from my physical ability and strength. I realised that one of the belief systems that drove my life was that I am only good enough if my body is able to perform the way it always has been. I had to learn how to ask for help without the irritation and the guilt that I could not do things on my own. I had to learn that I deserve other people's care and love. More than that, I had to discover what self-love looked like when all I could do was judge myself for the place that I found myself in. The toughest lesson that is possibly still ongoing for me was how to embrace all of this in order to make my decisions from a healthy loving place even when I am anxious and uncertain. This is a journey that takes lifelong commitment to self.

> I skip forward a few years and find myself in a different area of my life and my marriage. For the past four years our lives as individuals and our relationship had been marked by a strong sense of survival. We were becoming conditioned to survive life, our children's health (constantly being in hospital due to their low immune systems) and it seemed we were surviving our relationship too.

By this time Luca and Emma were four and two years old respectively and our lives were characterised by many nights in hospital and many days with sick kids at home while maintaining our professions on an upward curve. To give some context, more often than not, premature babies grow up to be children with a low-functioning immune system up to the age of about six years old and then the immune system seems to function similarly to that of other kids the same age. Thus a common cold became pneumonia in a few days in our household. This brought anxiety of a different kind. There was the concern for our children's health and then there were the logistics around who would work from hospital and who would go to the office and home to the other child who was not in hospital. Both of us were juggling the emotional, practical and physical discomfort to the best of our ability.

One of the unintended consequences was that we were so focused on the "how" of daily life that we lost sight of the "us" and what that meant during this season of our lives. We came to a point in our relationship that we could not hear each other through the fear, the fatigue and the prolonged anxiety of what was now "normal" in our lives. We tried date nights and argued through every single date night for months. We tried weekends away and for longer than I care to remember we spent those "romantic" weekends fighting with each other. We hit a rock-bottom low on the weekend that marked our seven-year wedding anniversary.

I recall standing in a beautiful suite with stylish interior that overlooked vineyards and valleys, screaming at my husband in a way that I have never communicated with anyone in my life. And as I was observing myself behaving in a way that disgusted me about myself, something happened.

I realised that I did not like who I was in our relationship any more, and if I did not like me I was not completely sure how my husband could like me. (He had his own realisations but that is his story to share.) That Sunday night we sat together and asked the question that was important to both of us. "Do we still love each other?" or had the last four years changed us so much that we did not recognise who we were as people or as a couple any more?

To my deep gratitude the answer was "yes, we do love each other ... but right now we do not know how to be together." And so the journey back to our relationship began. We went to see a psychologist whom we both love and trust and we discovered a few hard facts.

- Our relationship goal was my and our children's survival. We had to find a new goal that was as important and powerful to both of us, seeing that I was healthy and our children were on their way to becoming stronger.

- A big relationship assumption: If we can manage and survive the big things, the small things are automatically taken care of. Not true. We had to develop a different relationship resilience that included the importance of the small things again (the things we considered small).

- I cannot decide anything for my husband (or anyone else for that matter). This seems really obvious, yet there was a part of me that thought I knew "best".

- When we observe our own patterns we can identify our relationship patterns quicker and start listening to each other long before we have to scream. We had to remember to listen to hear, rather than listen to answer.

I think it is about now that I should mention that my husband served as my rock and anchor. I know for sure that I would not have been able to live through these experiences in a positive, embracing way if he had not been walking firmly by my side. I refer to him and our relationship a lot in these pages as the lessons are great and the gifts of our partnership are rich.

I purposefully share this part of my story because the anxiety of potentially losing the person I love was scary, unknown and I had to look inside myself all over again to find awareness and growth and do it from a healthy space even though I was anxious about the outcome.

Today I find myself being a Life, Business and Agile coach. A facilitator and trainer. A person who shares my purpose with as many people as I can in order to remind us all that anxiety might not be pleasant but it is real, part of our daily lives and possible to embrace.

During the process of writing this book, I was given the opportunity to practise what I preach in a very real way. As I went for my regular six-monthly check-ups, the doctor discovered a mole that had to be removed. From the date of removal to the date of receiving the results was a full seven long days. I got to sit next to the uncertainty and look for the possibilities in the not knowing. I got to choose to be grateful for what I have, to embrace the anxiety and speak at Cancer talks while I had no answer on my results. I got to feel anxious and not let it own me. The results came back negative and I got to be grateful and joyful all over again.

Cancer is a great gift; it is only the packaging that sucks.

I live the life of becoming with as much awareness as I can. Sometimes I do it skilfully and sometimes I really do it unskilfully and then I have a new opportunity to grow. I hope to continuously grow in awareness. I have since been clear of cancer for five years. My gratitude has no boundaries and I hope to share this model with all in order to transform our anxieties into personal and professional success.

The one thing no-one can take away from us or do for us is how we choose. The one thing that is important to know is: From what place and space inside of us do we make our choices?

CHAPTER 2

Let's Look at Anxiety

2.1 What is anxiety?

The answer ... Normal.

"Anxiety is a result of behaviour. Everyone experiences anxiety to some degree. And most people have panic attacks at some point in their lives. So anxiety is not bad. It is just a physiological, psychological and emotional outcome when we behave in an apprehensive manner."[2]

So, if anxiety is so normal, why is it so scary? And in that lies the answer. To feel and be anxious is a constant way of being that has the ability to impact our quality of life as well as the quality of decisions we make on a daily basis. It is true that everyone experiences anxiety at some point in their lives, yet we often numb the experience, ignore it, run away from it or simply pretend that we have never experienced it. We judge the fact that we experience anxiety. I find that we believe that we should be unaffected by the lives we live. I borrow from Brene Brown and use some poetic licence when I say we think we should be unaffected by our lives and make them look effortless. And anxiety so does not fit this assumption of life.

When I was diagnosed the first time, I was terrified all the time, and my housekeeper gave me the most beautiful phrase that still lives with me today: "Annie," she said, "this is not more than you." And that is the purpose of this book. Anxiety becomes a problem, disorder, condition or any other medical term that you can think of, when it owns us and our behaviour. In the pages of this book, we are going to explore a method of embracing your anxiety and making it work for you. I say **a** way, and not **the** way, because I believe there are many tools out there that can support and help us. I have found this tool to be universal and diverse enough to apply to all ages, from healthy teenagers to terminally ill people. Take out of this what works for you and blend it with the tools you already have.

To embrace our anxiety is a journey. It is daily practice until it becomes a way of living. Like most things of importance and value it requires commitment to one's self and the process. The "silver bullet" lies in the fact that we can choose every day until such time that the choices we make become our way of being. There are exercises in the book that can help you on your journey and I suggest you use them as often as you can based on where you are in your life's journey. Read the book and re-read it because when we grow we see different things of value based on where we are. We all experience stress and anxiety on this journey. It takes patience, willingness and discipline to embrace our anxiety. Having said that, it is totally doable.

Every person responds differently to anxiety due to our internal processes around the situation and/or our emotional reactions to certain situations, be they internal or external. Different people might perceive the same situation with less or more anxiety.

Tucker–Ladd bring the additional view that even when we experience anxiety, stress or fear, there are times that it could be helpful and times that it is not helpful at all. It is reported that anxiety or tension is an essential survival signal of our body telling us that something is going wrong and we need to correct it.

We are often faced with two different experiences – one defined in reality and one defined in perception. The true and accurate warning of danger that resides in reality is one that we cannot do anything about as the situation cannot be changed. This situation refers to healthy fear that could save our lives or cause us to take action that could be helpful to our situation. The other side of the behaviour that resides in our perception is when our built-in alarm system goes off but we do not know what is wrong and we feel out of control. This situation refers to our different perceptions, belief systems and way of being in the world that cause us to experience fear.[3]

Before I continue, I think that in a book about embracing our anxiety, it would be irresponsible not to take a look at the clinical side of anxiety. I would therefore like to briefly touch on the aspect of Generalised Anxiety Disorder (GAD). I want to acknowledge the predisposition towards GAD in some people. When I look at the symptoms in the *Diagnostic and Statistical Manual of Mental Disorders* (DSM:V) around generalised anxiety disorder I find that at some point in our lives we all display some of the symptoms to a lesser or greater extent. The classification according to the DSMV that I want to highlight is the following: When ..."[t]he anxiety, worry, or physical symptoms cause clinically significant distress or impairment in social, occupational, or other important areas of functioning".[4] It is important to note that a person is diagnosed as suffering from Generalised Anxiety Disorder (GAD) only once he or she has been experiencing the relevant symptoms on most days over a six-month period. Should you have been diagnosed with GAD and read this book, I do believe you will find some value in the practical tools. I do also strongly suggest that no medication, therapy or counselling should be stopped based on the opinions, tools and research in this book.

It is helpful to discern the differences and the relationship between anxiety, stress and fear.

Stress

- "the adverse reaction people have to excessive pressures or other types of demand placed on them".[5]

- "the harmful physical and emotional responses that occur when the requirements of a job do not match the capabilities, resources or needs of the worker".[6]

- "indicate that the term stress is used in different ways depending on the person and the environment".[7]

- "gives a broader description of stress in that it includes a complex sequence of events".[8]

If we look at this in our daily lives, we understand that short-term stress can be a driving force and even a motivational factor to some people. Some people need a goal or a deadline to focus on while other people need time and space to focus. Again the important factor is not to judge it but understand what is real for you where stress is concerned. Prolonged stress can lead to chronic anxiety and burnout.

Anxiety

- "a vague unpleasant emotional state with qualities of apprehension, dread, distress, and uneasiness".[9]

- How anxiety is differentiated from fear is that anxiety is objectless.[10]

- "a feeling of worry, nervousness, or unease about something with an uncertain outcome."[11]

In all the research I have done and workshops I have run, the most pronounced causes for anxiety are uncertainty and complexity. It is something we have to navigate in our everyday lives no matter who we are. It impacts us if we are moms who have to raise our kids, if we are students trying to be successful at our studies, if we are young adults entering the workforce, if we are experienced professionals that want to achieve their best and if we are professionals heading for retirement and all the possibilities that brings. It is real and part of our interaction with the world around us.

Fear

In researching fear it has been found that fear is seen as:

- "similar to anxiety except that fear has a specific object".[12]

- "an unpleasant, often strong emotion caused by anticipation or awareness of danger and accompanied by increased autonomic activity."[13]

- "an emotion that is pre-programmed into all animals and people as an instinctual response to potential danger".[14]

You will notice that the moment we give the discomfort, worry and uneasiness of anxiety a name, we turn it into a fear. In this model I purposefully take the anxiety and turn it into a fear in order to give the brain more certainty to work with without forgetting about the underlying anxiety.

Before we get to the model, I introduce a few essential concepts that will give the model context and that will help with the integration of information. In the next few pages we are going to:

- understand what causes anxiety.

- make the connection between resilience and vulnerability.

- define HOPE in conjunction with trust.

- understand the difference between change and growth.

In doing the above (with some exercises as well) we make sure that from an information integration process we have a basic language that supports the model and how we apply it. Think of it as a warm-up session before the actual run.

2.2   What are the major causes of our anxiety?

If we know that anxiety is not something to be afraid of (and we will work a lot with choice and judgement later on) and it is a normal response to believing something could harm us, how do we embrace this uncomfortable feeling?

Neuroscience teaches us that the brain works better with any problem if it can put it into a language that the person can understand and interpret. In the next diagram (Figure 2.1) we are giving the brain a visual and a language to help us understand what we can do to embrace our anxiety and what some of the most obvious causes for our anxiety are.

When we look at Figure 2.1, we will see that some of the core contributors to anxiety are uncertainty and complexity (also seen in some of our research definitions). One of the key ways to embrace our anxiety, is to come back to the thing that causes our anxiety ... with hope. I know it sounds strange and counter-intuitive, but it works. The key ingredient is choice. To remember that we have a choice in life. I also discuss how we choose in the final chapter of the book as the one thing that allows us to embrace anxiety: to choose from hope. It might not be easy, it is often not comfortable or pleasant, yet it is one of the few things no one can do for us or take away from us.

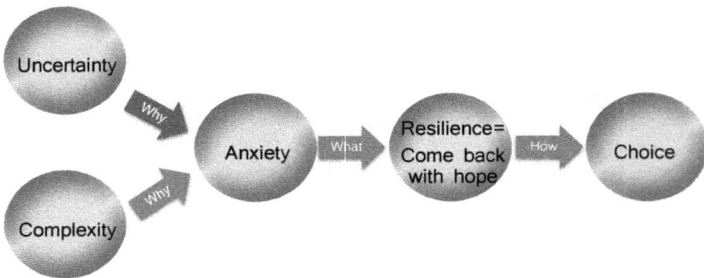

Figure 2.1: Some core contributors to anxiety

One of the skills we practise when we practise to get fit in embracing our anxiety is the ability to be truly comfortable with the discomfort that is caused by anxiety. Embracing anxiety through hope is not a passive "waiting for something to happen"; it is an active choice on how we engage with our anxiety and the world. In understanding more about the discomfort we take a look at complexity and uncertainty as two of the contributing factors to anxiety.

Complexity

When researching complexity it was ironic how little there was around a definition and how simple the definitions are. *Merriam Webster's*

Learners[15] *Dictionary* refers to complexity as "a quality or state of not being simple".

Upon further investigation Dave Snowden[16] has a model that describes various environments, organisations and systems and I found that this model was the most helpful in understanding why complexity adds to our anxiety levels in everyday life.

Table 2.1: The Cynefin Framework

UNORDERED DOMAIN	ORDERED DOMAIN	
Complex	**Complicated**	
Knowing only after the fact Flux and unpredictability No one right answer exists Unknown unknowns Many competing ideas Infinite range of possible outcomes Same thing re-appears in different form	Potentially knowable Repeating patterns can only be seen over a period of time. Cause and effect is discoverable but not immediately noticeable More than one right answer is possible Known unknowns Some form of recipe/pattern exists	INVISIBLE DOMAIN
Chaotic	**Simple**	
No knowing High turbulence No cause and effect perceivable Outcome is not predictable or explainable Crisis management No point looking for patterns High tension	Known Repeating patterns Consistent events Clear cause and effect The right answer exists Known knowns Cause and effect is predictable and repeatable	VISIBLE DOMAIN

Source: D. Snowden adapted by A. Bakkes[17]

Cynefin is a Welsh word that translates more or less as "the place of your birth and upbringing and the environment in which you live and naturally function within". In short, it is the world we find ourselves in on a daily basis.

Although this framework was designed for leadership decision making I found it very informative in terms of looking at my own life and what complexity means in my life. As human beings we are hard-wired to predict and prepare and we tend to dismiss the complex world in which we function which in turn increases our anxiety. Later we are going to look at what emotions we experience when we avoid this complexity. The irony is that we live in this complex space with interacting entities that unfolds as our life progresses and the only impact we have is the level of choice we exercise when we are aware of the complexity we face. I am borrowing from systems thinking and applying it to a more personal and individual context.

I will spend a little time on the four domains but will focus on how I have experienced complexity in various ways in my life.

- **Simple:** In a world where it is simple we have clear cause and effect that is easily identified by everyone and the right answer is often self-evident. I relate this simple space to my seven-year-old son and my process of parenting. There are clear boundaries of what we consider good manners in our home and the cause-and-effect of not behaving in accordance with those manners results in corrective action from myself or my husband. Not saying "please" and "thank you" will be followed by "how do we ask?" or any relevant form of reminder of what we believe the correct behaviour is. The boundaries are known and the cause-and-effect is predictable and clear. Anxiety and uncertainty are low in this space and once we know the boundaries, our confidence increases and decision making is of a high quality and fairly simple.

- **Complicated:** Complicated contexts might present multiple correct answers and there is a clear relationship between cause-and-effect, yet not everyone can see it. Again I can use my son in this space. When he plays a hockey match there are multiple ways in which he could play, pass and run that can result in a goal, yet he is not always aware of all the possibilities due to his inexperience. One of the key skills we use in a complicated environment is when we can see patterns over a period of time (experience) and make our decisions based on that information. A seasoned hockey player will be experienced in all the various moves that could lead to a goal and outwit the opponent because there is a known formula gained over time.

- **Complex:** In a complex context right answers cannot be figured out. It is the realm where the whole is far more than the sum of its parts and this is the world of unknown unknowns. Here we only understand why things happen in retrospect (and then sometimes we don't). It is in this space that we learn that our self-awareness is the key to being extraordinary. It is in this realm of unpredictability that we learn to allow life to unfold, be in the moment and make decisions as mindfully as possible with the information we have. It is here where we learn to trust our gut again and let go of what we perceive as control ... and if we don't, we live with sky-high levels of anxiety.

  I remember that when my son was born, it felt like there were hundreds of moving parts and no clear answers. There was the possibility that my son could contract cancer via the umbilical cord. The possibility that he would be disabled due to the premature birth. That I might not survive. A potential that my son would not survive. My coaching diploma for which I had to submit the final paper in a couple of weeks. And then there was the worry about how my husband was dealing with all of this.

  It is in this space of various moving parts with no clear outcome, answer or solution that I learned to embrace my anxiety and accept that being anxious is part of life, and how I choose to interact with it is the only thing I can control.

- **Chaotic:** When we shift into the chaotic context then there is no point in looking for the right answers and the cause-and-effect is impossible to determine because it changes constantly. I associate this with a few times in my life. I remember the afternoon I was diagnosed with cancer for the first time. There were no answers, no recipe and things changed more than once a day. Another time that I had moments of chaos was when I started my own coaching practice and I had to figure it out as I went along. And the last association I have with moments of chaos is raising my children. What works today does not work tomorrow and they constantly change. Although these are only chaotic moments we tend to make really low-quality decisions from these places. Our decisions become more irrational and erratic in moments of chaos. I specifically refer to moments of chaos, and they do pass, and it is rare that we spend large amounts of time there, yet the impact on our decision-making skills is significant.

Uncertainty

As we can see under "complexity", a big part of complexity is fuelled by not being able to predict, plan and know. This is where complexity supports uncertainty and dovetails in increasing our anxiety in everyday life.

David Rock, the director of the Neuroleadership Institute, shares the following: "The only certainty is more uncertainty."[18] It is helpful to understand how our brains deal with uncertainty and this gives a lot of insight into why we find uncertainty so anxiety provoking.

Daniel Gilbert[19] teaches us that the uncertainty is a state where we lack information about what, where, how and when something will happen. He calls this an aversive state of being. In psychology, aversion therapy involves the use of unpleasant stimuli that induce changes in behaviour through punishment. No wonder the state of uncertainty is scary – our brain relates uncertainty to potential danger or punishment. Rock indicates that most of our expendable energy as human beings goes into reducing uncertainty in our lives and we do not always do it skilfully or with the desired effect that includes certainty.

Our brain is similar to a prediction machine. It uses all our senses to gain information, store and predict what needs to happen next.

This predictive capacity involves all our senses and most of our energy until the brain has retained some form of certainty. Gilbert adds to this by showing that uncertainty has two components: an informal component that indicates a deficit of knowledge and a subjective component that is a feeling of not knowing. Thus both our feelings and our thoughts are impacted negatively by uncertainty if we do not know how to embrace our anxiety.

During the course of this book, we are going to learn how to become comfortable with the discomfort of uncertainty and how to navigate uncertainty and complexity in a way that limits our anxiety and improves our interaction and decision making in the world.

The model that I present in this book is supported by four pillars and the sole purpose of these is to give us new thought patterns, language and awareness in order to become resilient and cultivate the skill of resilience.

2.3 Resilience: Coming back with hope

When we consider the impact of complexity and uncertainty on our anxiety, then understanding how resilience can decrease our anxiety leads us into how our decisions impact our anxiety and our lives.

In looking through the various scholarly articles that define resilience there seemed to be one theme that I could track across the various journals and papers and that is that: resilience is the way we as humans interact with events that impact and change our lives. Mostly the research refers to how we respond and interact with traumatic events or at least what we would perceive as difficult events. The research also indicates that resilience could manifest differently for different people in different experiences. When I combine the research with my personal experience I would like to present resilience for the purpose of this model as follows:

Resilience ...

- is to come back with hope to whatever situation it is that you are facing in your life at any given point in time.

- can be learned, practised and taught.

- is a way of being that develops the more you practise it.

- is in essence a choice.

I say this from deep personal experience that I have practised over the last seven years and it has remained true for me. Not always easy and simple, but true.

One of my first introductions to practising resilience was when Luca was born. He weighed 1 000 g. His first meal was 1 ml of expressed breast milk through a tube in his nose that lead to his stomach. For the first few days he received 1 ml per hour until he was strong enough to digest more. A lot of his progress was measured by his weight gain as this in turn would give him strength to grow and build his immune system. Through this process he would gain 10 g on day 1 and 10 g on day two and maybe 12 g on day three. On day four he would have a big poo nappy and he would lose 20 g and I would sob and then pull myself towards myself. This process continued for at least the first four weeks of his life. I learnt to accept what was in front of me and to continue with hope.

A further resilience-strengthening time was straight after my daughter Emma was born. She weighed 2 000 g and was much stronger than her brother and could breathe on her own. And when I held the little body that was attached to a whole bunch of tubes and monitors, and I knew I was heading for aggressive surgery to remove the cancer I felt pretty overwhelmed and hopeless. As I sat there feeling totally miserable and not knowing where I would get the strength from to do it all again (in fact questioning strongly if I had it in me to do this again), Luca (by this time two years old and healthy) came bouncing into neo-natal ICU bringing with him hope and joy that could not be ignored. There was my 1 000 g preemie full of life and eager to see his little sister. In that moment of humility I learnt that resilience without hope often shows up as numb determination.

Another resilience-in-training process in our lives showed itself when my husband faced retrenchment. At that time I was about 12 months into building my "life, business and Agile coaching" practice when we received finalisation on the decision that Tiaan (my husband) would be retrenched. He received a fair financial package and was looking at options which I did not necessarily see as viable or suitable for him (or should I say for the uncertain wife in me who stressed about income). In the process of my husband exploring new options, the financial and career uncertainty for him and the impact it had on us as a couple, and my still being in the building phases of my practice were really really scary. It took a few rounds of introspection before I realised that the element that caused my anxiety was the fact that I felt out of control. I could not choose for my husband, nor could I make him take a position that I thought was best for him. This introduced a whole different element of resilience … trust. I realised that the opposite of control was not out-of-control, but trust. And now I had to trust another person to make the best decision for himself and his family. There was the relief that the decision was not mine and then there was the hope and trust in my husband's abilities to be the best decision maker he could be. This type of resilience is the toughest when it comes to the people who are closest to us, for example, the trust that our children will choose well and that we can only be resilient in supporting them with the gifts that we bring.

My most recent in my ever-continuing resilience training was my weight-loss process. I made a whole lot of assumptions and some of them quite arrogantly. If I could survive cancer, I thought, surely I should be able to stick to a simple eating plan … assumption flawed. I went on longer, more frequent runs, ate less, but stubbornly could not stick to a healthy eating plan. I became quite despondent. After about eighteen months of trying to lose weight the way I did when I was twenty, I realised that I had to see what was in front of me.

The old ways did not work any more, I was now a forty-two-year-old woman who had to look at her body in a different way. That in itself was uncomfortable and then I realised what some of the research had already told me. True resilience is to be vulnerable. It is to look (in this case at my body) at life in a way that is open to what has changed, eager to see the possibilities and courageous enough to not get it right the first time. The choice to choose yet again. To clarify, I still take long runs and I eat far more healthily but eighteen months ago it was because I desperately wanted to lose weight, and now I do it because I only have one body and treating it with love and compassion is what fuels me. Again the outward manifestation looks the same but the place where I make the decision from is significantly different. The resilience in this matter? Choosing every day that I will drink more water and eat healthily even when I am anxious and uncertain. As mentioned, this is work in progress and some days I do it really well and other days I do it really "not well".

Resilience, vulnerability, and trust and hope

If we believe that resilience is to come back with hope, then we start looking at the similarities between resilience and vulnerability. Much of the research positions them as opposing factors, yet I believe that they are supporting factors in embracing anxiety and our lives.

Brene Brown links courage, wholeheartedness (living with courage) and vulnerability. She indicates that at the heart of being courageous is vulnerability and worthiness: "Facing uncertainty, exposure and emotional risks and knowing that I am enough".[20] Brown continues to indicate that we allow our fear and discomfort to become judgement and criticism and we forget about the courage to be vulnerable. I want to add that we forget about the courage to be resilient. Resilience that includes hope stands strong in the face of uncertainty, judgement and risks. It chooses to stay hopeful when life looks dark and that indicates that we are open and allowing, with deep trust in our own worthiness.

Carl Rogers supports the notion of being open in order to be helpful in any relationship by stating "... to withhold one's self as a person and to deal with the other person as an object does not have a high probability of being helpful."[21] Rogers also continues to acknowledge how difficult it is to show self-acceptance and believe in our own worthiness through his research: "Now, acceptably to be what I am, in this sense, and to permit this to show through to the other person, is the most difficult task I know and one I never fully achieve."[22]

Brown goes further to indicate that: "Vulnerability is the core of all emotions and feelings. To feel is to be vulnerable. To believe vulnerability is weakness is to believe that feeling is weakness."[23] I want to add to that statement that hope is the feeling that differentiates us. Hope is the feeling at the core of resilience and growth. And with the research at hand combined with personal experience I believe that self-trust, the belief that we are worthy and hope are the ingredients to help us face any and all of life's challenges in the most real way possible. We have learnt that one of the things we all value is being real. "I have come to recognise that being trustworthy does not demand that I be rigidly consistent but that I be dependably real."[24]

When we speak about these ways of interacting with the world around us, it is hope that allows us possibility and joy even when we are anxious. Hope is not passive, Merriam Webster defines hope as "to expect with confidence" or "to cherish a desire with anticipation". What amazed me when I did the research is that the word HOPE finds its archaic roots in TRUST. How amazing that the two things that enable and inspire resilient living have their roots within each other. To take this a step further, hope is not the belief that everything will work out perfectly. Hope is the active trust that things will work our perfectly for you. If I did not have cancer, I would not have been able to write this book.

The opposite of control is Trust

Inspired by DoRa and Dr. M. Ungerer

Hope recognises the reality that failure happens, success is not assured, the laws of physics don't change and prudence is needed to discern when to persevere — and when to pivot. Hope doesn't demarcate a linear path, but it does guide us through twists and turns. Hope views the glass as half full, not half empty. Hope supports realistic optimism, a necessary component of success.[25]

We embrace our anxiety and build trust through making our decisions with increased awareness and from love, gratitude and hope. It is being able to feel hopeful that enables us to make everyday decisions with joy and if we do this with every seemingly small decision, the seemingly big decisions take care of themselves. We will learn in the pages of this book that feeling is the one thing that allows us to be resilient and that opens us to understanding our choices. "Every time we allow ourselves to lean into joy and give into those moments of feeling, we build resilience and we cultivate hope."[26]

You will notice that resilient people are not exempt from feeling deeply unsettling and negative emotions. It is your level of self-awareness and practice of choice that allows you to show up more resilient in every situation. We are entering the part of the book where the tools that enable us to practise resilience and choice are explained as well as "how to" practise using these tools. At the end of the day, when we embrace our anxiety it is one of the most liberating choices we can make again and again and again.

2.4 Growth vs change

When we did culture work in corporates, I learnt from my friends at the Star Performance Group that it is possible to change without growing, but that it is not possible to grow without changing. It is possible to make the same choice from a different angle and think that we have changed, but it is the same behaviour dressed in a different manifestation. Our level of judgement plays a role in whether we grow or merely change.

If we want to facilitate growth in others (via leading, loving, parenting, guiding friendships or work relationships) we have to grow internally, and while this is painful it is also enriching. Carl Rogers teaches us about the essence of growth as a human being: "The degree to which I can create relationships which facilitate the growth of others as a separate person is a measure of the growth I have achieved in myself."[27] It seems that one of the first steps towards suspending our judgement is to grow.

In looking at the model below, it starts with awareness and moves to acceptance and then to action and achievement. Under the topic of "suspended judgement" we will focus on the awareness and acceptance steps. When we focus on "behaviour" later in the book, we will focus on action and achievement. In order to suspend our judgement, the first aspect we are going to look at is awareness.

Figure 2.2: Change and Growth

Source: Star Performance Group 1999-2016

Awareness

The difference between being average and excellent in anything we do is our level of awareness. In the case where we refer to judgement, we refer specifically to our level of self-awareness that is of the utmost importance in order for us to start the journey towards growth and in some cases influence our environments.

Brene Brown describes self-awareness as the ability to see ourselves for who we are, until we change. Brown continues to say that at the core of meaningful experiences with self (and then others) lies the ability to be vulnerable with self.[28] In my coaching practice I have found that the thing we want the most is also one of the things we fear the most and that is self-discovery. We fear it because we judge it. We are afraid that if we change, the person who we used to be was "wrong all this time". Before we can grow we need to be able to see ourselves. Sometimes we have not even met the real us ... sometimes we are not even sure who we are under all our armour and masks. Self-awareness is the first step towards self-acceptance and self-acceptance decreases anxiety.

> The difference between average and excellent is our level of self awareness.
>
> A. Bakkes

As humans we have the tendency to define things by what they are not. This is especially true when we define emotional experiences.[29] The moment we start using language like "I should have, could have, should have known, wished I knew better, should have done more, known more or better" we find ourselves squarely in the land of self-judgement ... the opposite of self-awareness.

One of the first challenges we are going to face in the exercises of this book, is to be real with ourselves. It is part of the journey in embracing anxiety, the looking in the mirror and seeing what is really there. Ironically, when I give talks, have coaching sessions or run workshops people without fail comment on the fact that they can relate to the material, the content and me because it is real. We crave real connection yet we often find it hard to be real with ourselves. It is far easier to judge ourselves than look at ourselves with compassion and realness.

In our "warm-up" phase we are going to do two exercises. To call them practices is actually more descriptive as it starts to open our minds, thinking and feeling to how we interact with the world from an awareness and acceptance perspective. My suggestion would be that you do these two exercises daily for a period of 28 days and then review what you have discovered. By then it should gently become part of your thinking and feeling.

Some sections of this book have POWER start exercises as way of describing the practice, some sections have summaries at the end and still others have different exercises, so there is not a flow of stock standard exercises. They are all relevant to that specific section of the book.

✎ Exercise 1: POWER start

We are going to use a POWER start (borrowed from Agile Coaching Institute 2015 and adapted by A Bakkes). A power start helps us to see the relevance in what we do. It is often used to plan meetings, but I found it useful to structure our exercises this way to make them more meaningful. The tasks in Exercise 1 are designed to:

Purpose	• Practise our level of awareness of judgement of self and others • Become aware of the feelings, situations and anxiety that accompany our judgement
Outcome	• Increased awareness of when we practise judgement of self and others and the impact it has on our thoughts, feelings and actions
What is in it for me?	• The ability to see our own judgements and those of others in order to make higher quality decisions that are not informed by anxiety and/or fear

Engage	• You are required to engage your suspended judgement, open mind and curiosity during this exercise
Resources (you will require)	• Uninterrupted reflection time
	• Willingness
	• Time to think (10 min per day)
	• Awareness
	• Observation as a practice

This is a "being and observing" practice, it is not a "doing" practice (in preparation for some mindfulness observation that comes later in the model). It requires you and your attention to yourself.

Instruction: During your day start taking notice of the following without any attempt to change anything. Purely become aware of what is requested to the best of your ability.

Start noticing (try not to judge) when you use self-judging language (also known as negative self-talk) for example:

I should have had the answer

I should have known

I should have ......

Why did I not ......

Take notice of your feelings and in what circumstances you are when you feel them. Please try not to judge that you are feeling or what you are feeling ... just observe.

Take 10 uninterrupted minutes per day to reflect on yourself – nothing else, just yourself. (Uninterrupted means no phones, no books, nothing but you and your thoughts.)

Acceptance

"Of course there is no formula for success except, perhaps,
an unconditional acceptance of life and what it brings."[30]

When I speak to people about acceptance, the conversation often carries the energy of "defeatedness" and that is not at all what I mean when I talk about acceptance.

"Acceptance in human psychology is a person's assent to the reality of a situation, recognising a process or condition (often a negative or uncomfortable situation) without attempting to change it, protest, or exit."[31]

The key phrase that talks to me in the above definition is the "recognising", the seeing what is there. Recognise means to acknowledge the existence of. That is it, nothing more, nothing less, just to see what is there.

Acceptance
≠
Agreement

DoRa

We often mistake acceptance for agreement yet it does not have to be the case. Once a glimpse of self-awareness is present one can start differentiating acceptance that does not by default include agreement. One of the limiting elements in the world of work is that we think we have to agree with the things we cannot control or influence. Accepting the things we do not agree with allows for higher levels of engagement and thinking. Hope for the future and acceptance of the present are not mutually exclusive.

As leaders, parents, friends and human beings this is one of the differentiating competencies. The ability to accept the situation, person, system and/or process for what it is and working with what is there. Once there is an element of acceptance there is more clarity to work with. The moment clarity steps in, our levels of anxiety come down due to the uncertainty that is reduced. Acceptance allows for flow in thinking and action.

In my coaching and workshops people have been asked to look at the things they judge most about themselves, their work situation, family and other. Once this judgement has been identified, they are asked to consider the possibility of accepting whatever it is that they might be judging. It is interesting how often people do not even consider the possibility of acceptance. If people can bring themselves to consider the possibility of acceptance, their entire being changes. People describe the possibility and action of acceptance as: "Being lighter, a sense of relief, becoming open to other possibilities, a feeling of clarity and the experience of a weight that has been lifted." In short, acceptance allows for hope to step in.

We have spoken about acceptance of what is, but what about self-acceptance? Self-acceptance is being loving and happy with who you are right *now*. It's permission to yourself to appreciate, validate, accept and support who you are at this moment. Some have the misconception that if you are happy with yourself you won't change things about yourself. This isn't true; you don't have to be unhappy with yourself to know and actively change things you don't like. A current **example** for me is that I want to lose 6 kg. I can accept that I want to lose this weight and fit into some of my clothes again. This acceptance allows me to see more than just the excess weight and the clothes I do not fit into. I do however not have to agree with the way I look at the moment. The acceptance of what is gives me the courage to get onto the scale and start making practical changes to my eating habits and exercise regime.

Of course, life will bring many challenges, and it's not easy to embrace them when we're suffering and wishing those things had never happened. But if we start cultivating acceptance in our lives right now, we'll likely cope with future crises in a different way and view them from a different perspective. We will accept instead of resisting.

"The curious paradox is that when I accept myself just as I am, then I can change." Carl Rogers

---

✎ Exercise 2: Practise acceptance

Purpose	• Practise our level of acceptance of the things we judge
	• To become familiar with the impact on our insights when we practise acceptance
Outcome	• Experience of how acceptance (with or without agreement) increases our ability to gain insight and improve our ability to grow
What is in it for me?	• Increased awareness and ability to choose to grow based on insights gained
Engage	• You are required to engage your writing and reflective skills
Resources (you will require)	• Uninterrupted reflection time
	• Willingness
	• Time to journal (10 min per day)
	• A pen, pencil, journal or electronic device to journal on.

This exercise works best if it is done in a journal and revisited on a weekly basis as we tend to obtain insight when we walk around with the thoughts in our heads for a few weeks. Notice how your level of awareness has grown since your last exercise.

Instruction: Journal the following questions on a regular basis (2–3 times a week)

What does acceptance look like to you? (This includes how you know when you accept and when you are accepted.)

at work

at home

as a parent

as a leader

of self

When will you know that you are accepted?

What behaviour and actions will you see or not see?

When will you know that you fully accept?

How will you behave or not behave?

Right now in my life: What is the hardest thing for me to accept? What about that ... am I judging?

CHAPTER 3

The Model

I am going to start this chapter with the end picture in mind. I am going to present you with a summarised version of the model and form of a "cheat sheet" that has all the key elements of the Embracing Anxiety Model and processes. Then I will expand on the steps and give them some more context and then we will launch into unpacking the model one step at a time. At any time you can refer back to this "cheat sheet" (and I will take you through where we are in the model as a reminder of where we find ourselves).

The "cheat sheet" is a quick reference in recipe form to remember how to embrace our anxiety. The next few paragraphs give a slightly more informed explanation and then the detail of each step is described in the following pages.

How to embrace my anxiety "Cheat Sheet"

1. Become aware of when you judge (Suspended Judgement)

    a. What judgement towards self and others am I aware of?

    b. Can I accept myself and others, knowing that acceptance does not equal agreement?

    c. Ask ... what am I attached to?

    d. What is another way I can look at this?

    e. When I use "should, could, must have" replace it with "next time I will"

2. Mindfully observe what is there (Observation)

    a. Think about your thinking. Am I changing or am I growing?

    b. What do I become aware of when I mindfully observe without fixing?

    c. What is possible from here?

3. Invite love (Love)

    a. What about me can I love?

    b. What about my judgement can I love?

    c. Practise practical love.

4. Practise Gratitude (Gratitude)

    a. Become aware of what you are grateful for every day.

    b. Want what you already have.

    c. Share your gratitude, tell someone.

5. Give it a Name (Embrace your anxiety)

    a. Discover the drive behind your anxiety. What am I afraid of?

    b. Invite courage and gentle honesty. This creates certainty in the mind

    c. Be courageous enough to identify your fear. (Do you want to walk around with spinach in your teeth the whole day or do you want to see it in the mirror first before starting the day?) Through identifying your own fear, you remove the spinach from your teeth and enable certainty towards a goal.

6. Identify the Belief System (BS) that supports your fear.

    a   Is this belief system true?

    b   What about this belief system limits you?

    c   Now that you know ... what is possible?

    d   Create a liberating belief system that replaces the limiting belief system. Choose from Hope. It remains a choice.

7. How do my body and emotions react to anxiety?

    a   Where in my body do I carry my anxiety?

    b   What physical symptoms is my body experiencing?

    c   How kind am I towards my body? (remember to suspend judgement)

8. How do I behave when I am anxious?

    a   Impact feedback: When you ...... I feel ......

    b   What behaviour can you observe?

    c   What fear informs your behaviour?

    d   How does this behaviour serve me?

    e   Next time ... how do I want to behave?

9. Choice: What do I choose with the tools that I have?

    a   What support do I need to choose?

    b   From what place inside me am I choosing? Fear or Hope?

    c   Give yourself permission to choose.

    d   Practise to choose from Hope and with compassion

    e   What do I need to put my choice into action?

In order to apply the model we need a language and some positive habits that will support us in getting the best out of the model in the short and long term. The above is a recipe that summarises the model in a way that is practical and usable, yet we have to understand the detail of the process to apply it with insight and growth.

3.1 The four pillars of the model

Suspended Judgement: I start the framework with suspended judgement because I have learned though personal experience and research that judgement (towards self and others) is one of the key things we use to make life more certain, yet in doing so, we send our anxiety sky high. If we can suspend our judgement we can see what is and embrace it rather than fear it.

Observation: In order to grow and not only change we need to be able to boost our new awareness with acceptance of what is. Observation is the ability to think about our thinking, mindfully observing our patterns and thus lowering our anxiety.

Love: One of the alchemists of anxiety to hope is practical expression of love to self and then others. To invite the compassion to see what is there without judgement and then lovingly act in a way that is present, collaborative, understanding and without fear. Practising love lowers our anxiety.

Gratitude: It turns out that gratitude is the real magic of embracing anxiety. If we can identify and practise gratitude, be appreciative of what we already have, then we can share our gratitude and change ourselves and the world around us. Gratitude does not occur without discomfort but often in the midst of it.

The first four elements of this model are about how we interact with the world that helps us to minimise our anxiety and increase our confidence, sense of self-worth and increase the quality of how we apply the model with insight in the next five steps.

3.2 The five steps in the model

Identify your fear: There is a difference between stress, anxiety and fear. The key element is that fear has an object and anxiety is objectless. If we give our anxiety a name, we give our brain and body the best possible chance of long-term tools to embrace what is there.

If we can see it, we can choose to change it.

Observe the belief systems that support our fear (anxiety): Belief systems are assumptions that become facts in our lives and that we use to make our decisions. (It is here where we apply suspended judgment and observation in order to see what is and to enable growth.) We have the power to choose new enabling belief systems that invite hope.

How do our body, brain and emotions react when we are anxious? It is here that we have to apply observation in order to see what is there, what clues our bodies give us and what tips our emotions give us to look at the root cause of our anxiety (and/or fear). We learn how our brain has the possibility to change if we choose and practise to change it (neuroplasticity). We start practising how to actively change our belief systems, recognise our emotions and listen to our bodies in order to embrace our anxiety.

Our behaviour when we are anxious: In this stage of our model we get to practise all the tools and tips we have learnt up to this point. Behaviour is the outward manifestation of our anxiety, belief systems, our emotions and how our brain interprets the world. Our behaviour is the last sentence of an entire internal conversation, yet only the last sentence is displayed in actual behaviour. Here we learn how to choose our behaviour, feel the feelings that inform our behaviour and be conscious about what we do and how. (Again we invite suspended judgement, we observe what we do, we practise love and gratitude in our behaviour and we are aware of which belief systems we invite during which behaviour.) We invite action with purpose.

How do we choose? It seems odd that we end with choice, seeing that the entire model and way of engagement is based on the fact that we have and can employ choice. We conclude our model by giving ourselves permission to choose, to become aware of where we make our decisions from and if these decisions are healthy, high quality and sustainable for how we want to be. By remembering that we have choice, we truly embrace our anxiety and choose to live and make our choices in a way that allows for hope in our lives. We reach achievement with focus and consciousness.

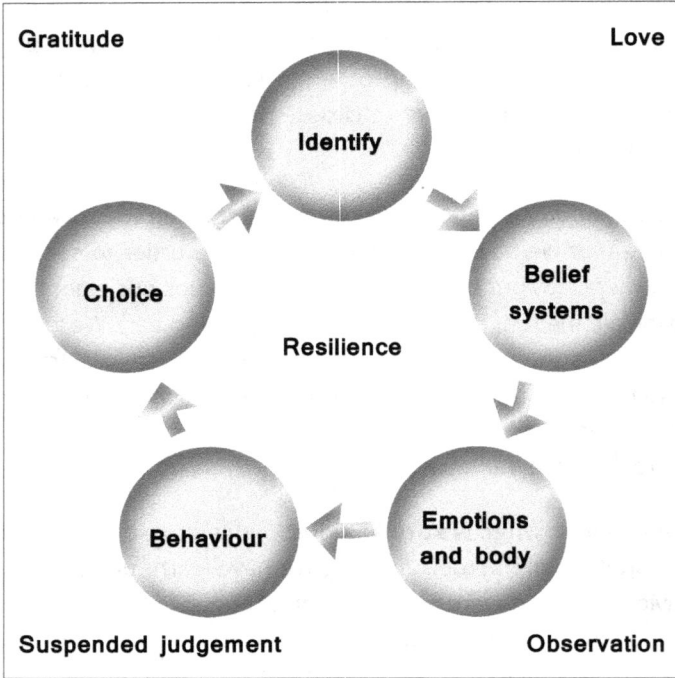

Figure 3.1: Model: Embracing Anxiety[32]

CHAPTER 4

The Four Pillars of the Model

4.1. Suspended judgement

"... to be that self which one truly is"[33]

This part of the process ties in directly with the part where we discussed the value of awareness as we well as acceptance. Once we have higher levels of awareness can start seeing our judgement for what it is, hence the bit of "warm-up" work that we did before we dive into suspended judgement.

I would like to acknowledge that I am not sure that we ever reach a place of "no judgement" on this human journey. I have however experienced and witnessed in life and in the workshops and coaching I have done while applying this model that once the awareness of our own judgement is increased and suspended, even if only for a short while, it changes the way we look at the world and our anxiety. If we are able to suspend our judgement to the best of our ability we tend to see the world for what it is and not only what our judgement limits us to see.

From a language perspective the dictionaries tell us the following about judgement:

- The ability to judge, make a decision, or form an opinion objectively, authoritatively, and wisely, especially in matters affecting action; good sense; discretion

- The forming of an opinion, estimate, notion, or conclusion, as from circumstances presented to the mind

- Judgement is the evaluation of evidence to make a decision. Informal: Opinions expressed as facts.

From the workshops, individual and group coaching sessions I have lead, I have come to understand that there is a whole different understanding in the world around judgement other than what is presented in the dictionaries. When I run an "Embracing Anxiety" workshop and I ask people to write down the words that come up when I say the word "judgement", these are the most common words that people use to describe judgement:

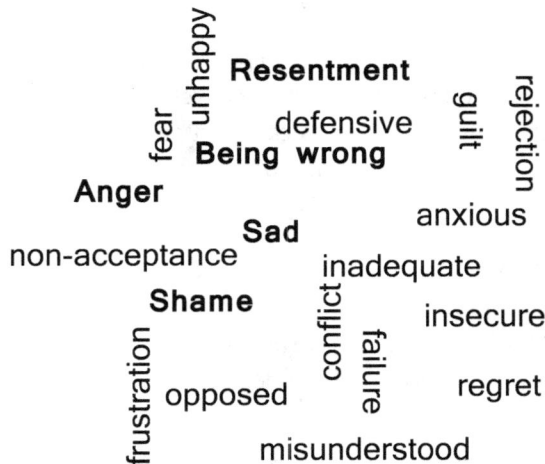

Figure 4.1: Common words that people use to describe judgement

Once I really mindfully reflected on this information that seems to repeat itself, no matter where I find myself in the world, I realised that in order for our brains to understand the feeling of judgement better, it would be helpful to understand some of the factors that influence our judgement. The ONE most important contributing factor towards our judgement of self and others is our attachment to:

- a situation
- the outcome of that situation
- a person
- how people perceive us and
- where we find ourselves at that point in our lives.

Our level of attachment
to the outcome

=

Our level of judgement

=

Our level of fear

A. Bakkes inspired by DoRo

Attachment

Attachment can be seen as the value, importance and weight you put on something, some situation or the outcome of something. The higher we value something the higher our level of judgement.

Our level of attachment to a person, job, situation or event is a telltale sign of our level of judgement. Our judgement is particularly influenced by our fear, our attachment, our need for and our perception of what is "right". Our judgement often tells us more about our fears, views of the world, insecurities and wounds than it tells us about the person, process or situation that we are judging.

When we look at change of any kind in the world and the judgement and fear that the change ignites in people, it is evidence of how our attachment impacts our decision making and effectiveness. Depending on our life's journey and story we will have different attachments to different situations.

In the world of work, judgement as a limitation in the form of attachment to the outcome manifests in many ways. One of my clients, a CIO of a big company, had a strong fear of being perceived as incompetent amongst his fellow executive members. Both his fear of being perceived as incompetent and his attachment to being perceived as competent drove a lot of his choices and behaviour in the workplace. This manifested clearly during a very large and expensive systems implementation programme in the company. Due to the financial investment in the new system, the executive team required detailed updates on a regular basis. As the CIO it was this person's role to lead, guide and enable the people in his team to deliver this programme. Due to his need to be perceived as competent, he refused to invite any of his technical staff to the executive meetings for fear that he might look incompetent and "not knowing". This lead to late-night meetings for updates from his team and staff. This fear resulted in his over-involvement in the detailed activities of his team which limited him in his actual delivery and role as a senior leader. It took some failure, people resigning due to micro-management and missed deadlines for him to realise that his actual fear was becoming a reality by his not doing what he was required to do.

Once the self-awareness around his judgement increased and he could see himself and his behaviour clearly, he started choosing differently. Once the insights occurred due to awareness and acceptance of what he could see, he chose to change things. He restructured his team internally in terms of programme reporting and invited the specialists to report to the executive team once a month in order to communicate the technical tracking, delivery and implementation, while he gave feedback on the finances and vendor relations. Once he realised that his judgement around his incompetence limited his achievement he started looking at what was really there and not only at what his judgement allowed him to see.

Personally, I like to think that my attachment to most things is low, yet do not tell me how to raise my children. I am still very attached to what "a good mother" looks like. This attachment trips me up in more ways than one and I have to consciously look at my decisions and ask myself where I am making them from. Am I making them from fear, a parenting wound, from my attachment to what "good" looks like or from a healthy balanced place? I have to ask myself more than once a day and be as aware and as kind to myself as I can.

I am also observing (discussed in the next section in this book) that I am quite attached to writing this book and making sure it is the best it can be. Right now I do not think I am attached to what people will say (unless I am hiding from myself and that is also possible) but I am attached in the sense that the book be "good enough". A theme that is still part of my journey … I will percolate on this as I continue writing.

Exercise 3: Practise becoming aware of our attachment

Purpose	• To become aware of the things, outcomes, situations and/or behaviour that we are attached to • How does being attached to something impact our thoughts and behaviour?
Outcome	• Become aware of how our attachment influences our behaviour, thoughts, feelings and decisions • To gain insight into why we are attached to the above discoveries
What is in it for me?	• The ability to see how some attachments limit us • The information to see what is there and possibly accept or change it
Engage	• You are required to engage your courage, acceptance, writing and reflective skills
Resources (you will require)	• Uninterrupted reflection time • Willingness and courage • Time to journal (10 min per day) • A pen, pencil, journal or electronic device to journal on

Let's become aware of what it is that we are attached to in our lives (work and personal). It is helpful to use a journal when doing this exercise as this often delivers some surprises. This exercise requires courage to really look at ourselves and it is totally liberating to see ourselves in a different light. Try not to judge what you discover, but to be curious to find out more ... a little like a treasure hunt.

Instruction: Take note of the following states and write them down as and when you become aware of them.

- Notice what you are attached to. Examples:

  o Being right, doing it right

  o Being perfect

  o Being the perfect ... parent, boss, partner, and more ...

  o My child must ...

- Observe how you behave when you are attached to the outcome of something, someone or a situation. Please invite your self-awareness.

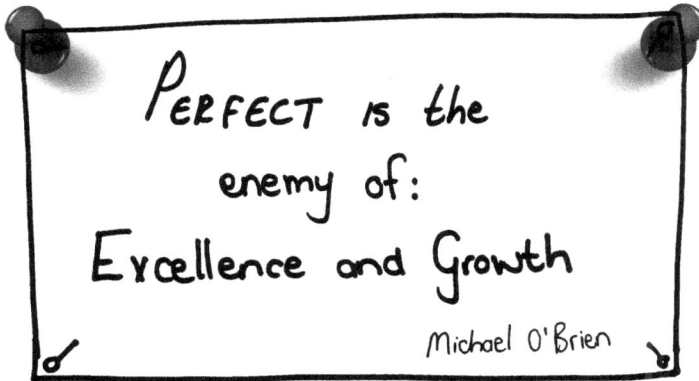

PERFECT is the enemy of: Excellence and Growth

Michael O'Brien

The limiting element of judgement

"Judgement exacerbates disconnection"[34]

I know that we judge as another way to make life more certain, yet the same thing we do to "keep us emotionally safe" is the thing that limits our insight and our ability to see what is there. David Rock describes it as a fixed world view that does not allow us to see the world through others' eyes. This limits us in a way that we can only see our view and thus miss out on other potential possibilities of choice and being.[35]

We also use our judgement to make decisions that previously worked in similar situations, without taking the uniqueness of this current situation into consideration and this leads to limiting decisions and actions based on past experience. (Falling back on old solutions keeps us feeling certain and limits our thoughts and solutions.) This way we try and fit our solutions into previous recipes of "what worked" and that has the potential to limit our growth. It is natural to repeat successful decisions of the past. All we need to do is invite what we have learned up to now to ensure that we are seeing what is really there.

When I judge
all I can see
is my
judgement

A. Bakkes inspired by C. Rogers

We see the world through our own filters and belief systems created through our life's journey, experiences, observations and traumas. If our level of self-awareness is low our level of judgement tends to be high. One of the things that differentiate leaders from the pack is their level of self-awareness and how they apply that in their various leadership styles.

We tend to judge the world through the same filters that we use to judge ourselves. The elements we judge the most in ourselves tend to be those elements that we judge most harshly in other people. Due to this judgement through our own filters, we miss the opportunity to see what is really there and not just what we are observing through and due to our judgement of the person and the situation. (When we talk about love later in the book, we have the opportunity to change this way of thinking.)

We lead and mislead people through our frame of judgement and belief systems. More often than not we judge due to fear that enhances our anxiety and informs our decisions and behaviour. When we are anxious there is more electrical activity in the brain which makes it harder to perceive subtle signals. There is too much noise in our thoughts for us to hear and gain insights.[36] It is insight and seeing what is real that enable us to connect with people and make the best decisions and have the most impactful relationships. Rogers refers to these judgements as internal concepts and indicates that each of these concepts limits what can be in a relationship.[37] When we are brave enough to look at our own judgement, about what is in front of us, we have the ability to start seeing what is really there and thus choose to make different decisions.

In a training session I attended, Michael O'Brien[38] taught me the following. The moment we tell our brains the word or phrase "should", the part of our brain that does not recognise time as a concept continues to try and fix the situation. (Which it can't, as it happened in the past.) It's these kinds of thoughts that keep us awake at night as the brain is trying to solve something it can't. A way to give our brain the opportunity to fix the problem is to use the phrase "next time". This way we give our brain a problem to solve that is in the future and possible to do. When we continue having "next time" conversations with ourselves around the same topic and behaviour repeatedly we are creating behavioural patterns that need some investigation.

Key questions you can ask yourself:

- What about yourself, the situation or the person in front of you is it that you judge?

- What is your level of attachment to that which you are judging?

- Is it possible to accept this that you are judging (keeping in mind that acceptance does not equal agreement)?

- If this is what it is, can you see it for what it is?

- If you know this judgement is not the truth, what is the next step?

- If I can accept this person, situation or element about myself, how does my behaviour change?

Note: It remains a choice to be less attached to something or not. It is more important to see the attachment for what it is and understand where you are making your choices from than changing the attachment.

4.2 Observation

Observation is the ability to observe your thinking. As David Rock says, it is the ability to "think about your thinking". Williams and Penmann build on this by saying that mindful observation is about observing our thoughts without criticism.[39] Being able to mindfully observe our thinking allows us to interact differently with the world. It enables us to see what is really there.

Another way of saying this is to take a step back from your thinking and gain a new perspective. It is during observation that we gain new insights into the same situation or feeling and we are able to make decisions that are not from anxiety. We often do not think about our thinking, we tend to go through the motions without being present to ourselves. Williams and Penmann make the differentiation between two states that we exist in. They call it the "doing mode", also known as our autopilot and "being mode" which refers to a state of reflective observation. I have observed that in the world of work and, upon reflection, in the western world at large, it seems that activity is rewarded above thinking. In one of my workshops I asked people what it is that they judge the most about their team's behaviour, and one person (a female lawyer) wrote "the weakness of inactivity". As a voice of our human system, she worded what a lot of managers in the corporate and entrepreneurial world believe. The challenge with this way of thinking and doing is that doing without reflection is mostly of a lower quality and with limited insight and quality. I want to go as far as to say that if we take more time to observe our thinking that results in choices of behaviour, we will have to do far less because our doing will be with focused intent, driven from conscious choice and of higher quality. I often hear from my clients "we have to do more with less" and they proceed to do what they are doing "harder and faster" because reflecting and feeling are not rewarded or just do not come to mind at all.

The trouble with doing more and harder without reflection is that it invites more anxiety due to additional pressure and more intense "autopilot" behaviour. How often have you gone through a meeting, a morning or a full day, not paying attention to what you are doing, but just doing to do? To the point that it is so automatic that we cannot recall what we did, said or decided, because we were too busy? I have to smile at the irony. This takes us right back to awareness of self. Mindful observation takes us out of a state of doing and puts us into a state of being. This gives us the opportunity to consciously choose our doing by the time we get there. It helps us to step outside of our mind's natural tendency to over-think, over-analyse and over-judge into a space of awareness of what is now and what is real in order to be more allowing of our thoughts. This alone helps us to be less anxious. If you are becoming anxious just thinking of being alone and observing with your thoughts, that is OK. Becoming quiet and observing our thoughts and feeling can be scary, until we practise it and see that that is all they are ... thoughts and feelings that we have the ability to choose with insight. Thoughts and feelings have the tendency to come and go and ultimately we have a choice as to how we interact with them.

Insight is strongly linked to observation and mindfulness. Have you often had a challenge or something to solve and the answer dawned while you were in the shower, or going for a run or when you had a conversation that was not related to your issue at all? Insight is the moment when things change internally and is our "aha" moment of self-insight. That moment of insight sparks a rush of adrenaline and dopamine and it leaves us excited and feeling great. This is one of the key elements that give us hope. Again, hope is one of our key elements of embracing our anxiety.

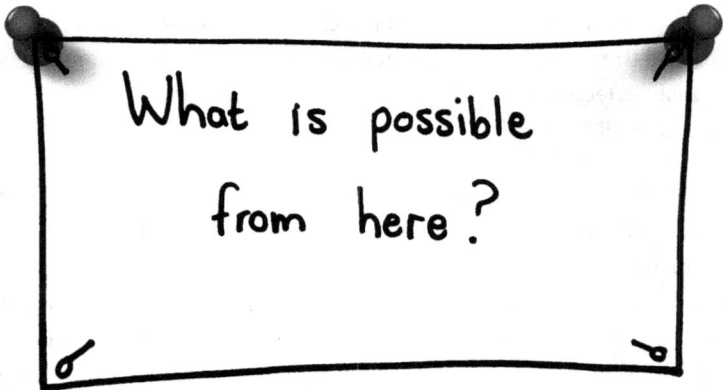

What is possible from here?

I personally faced a conundrum because I am an analytical logical thinker and became anxious when I could not solve some of my professional and personal problems through thinking about them. I gained insight when I read Williams and Penmann's view when they say that emotions are not problems to be solved, but rather feelings and emotions to be felt. They describe emotions as the background colour that is created when our mind fuses together all of our thoughts, raw feelings, impulses and bodily sensations to conjure up an overall guiding theme of a state of mind.[40] Mindful observation is to truly observe all of this as it happens and to be aware of it. Just describing emotions like we just did, again ties a golden thread to complexity and now we can see why. Our emotions are not one-dimensional at all but rather bundles of thoughts, feelings, bodily sensations and impulses to act. And here is where I pause, because when I observe this dance I can choose my actions with insight and conscious intent.

When we practise mindful observation it gives us the capacity to align our intentions and our actions. When we are in doing mode or autopilot our actions and our intentions are often not aligned. I am going to use a scenario with my husband (whom I dearly love) to illustrate this. I had the opportunity to travel to the USA and then again one week later to Sweden. Due to logistics and being in doing mode, I did not apply for my visa to go to Europe before I left for the USA. This meant that we had more or less six working days to apply for a Schengen visa. I want to be clear that my husband's intention was to help me and make this process as easy as possible knowing the work I had to do between the two trips.

We made sure that all the required paperwork was done before our appointment at the consulate. We were prepared and ready; the only outstanding thing was to have the relevant photographs taken for the visa application. I arrived from the USA the night before, I was eager to see my husband and children and to spend as much time with them as possible. The next morning we left the house later than we intended to and the following transpired. My husband wanted to leave earlier as he had an important report that had to go to a certain client that morning and he was pretty tired from looking after two children for ten days while I was away. We went in separate cars so that he could go to work after our appointment. By the time we arrived at the place where the photographs were to be taken he was both furious and despondent. His doing mode had already decided that our visa application would be turned down because we were late for our appointment, still had to have photographs taken and sit in line for our turn at the embassy and that his report would be arriving late at the client. I am sure we can all relate to this. His whole day was impacted by this pre-decided pattern of thinking. As it turned out, we were 15 minutes late for our appointment, we were the only people in the queue at that time and our visas arrived two days early.

This is just an everyday example of how we judge, pre-decide and live in doing mode. We have all been there – our situations just present themselves in different ways.

This brings us back to how we choose and how aware we are of our choices. The regions involved in our cognitive control, when we switch our train of thought, are activated prior to insight. The idea is to invite the self-awareness to our thinking. We think about certain problems, issues or challenges in a certain way and if we can become aware of our thinking, we can observe it (with as little judgement as possible) and choose to change our way of thinking. This takes as back to self-awareness and being aware of our experience. People who show more insight are the people who can observe their own thinking and thus change how they think, and their behaviour and then their choices. Again this brings us back to the importance of knowing and being aware of ourselves in order to make the best decisions we can at the time.[41]

One of the things we can control in order to remedy the anxiety that is caused by uncertainty, is our interpretation of the meaning of a situation and/or feeling. We have the ability to reappraise the situation if we take the time to observe, notice our patterns and see it for what it is instead of our judgement.

When we are stuck in our pre-determined thinking and high in judgement, our limbic system makes it very difficult to observe. Anxiety is not a bad thing. It is how we interact with it that is key. The challenge is not to become numb, avoid or not feel; it is to learn to feel the emotion, have as little judgement as possible, give it a name (through observation) and not act from it. Bottom line – feel the difficult and/or uncomfortable, even painful emotion, observe it and choose not to act from it.

It is here that the nucleus of our decision making lies. True mindful observation gives us the ability to be aware of what is happening in our inner and our outer world at the same time. The gap between what we perceive and where we think we should be trips us up because the focus remains on where we are not. Observation allows us to approach a situation without pre-conceived conclusions and allows for the magic of curiosity and discovery of what is.

When we start treating our thoughts as facts and a form of solidity rather than a temporary mental event, we tend to get stuck. It is really important to note that our thoughts and feelings are valuable, but they do not define us. They are part of us, part of a complex whole.

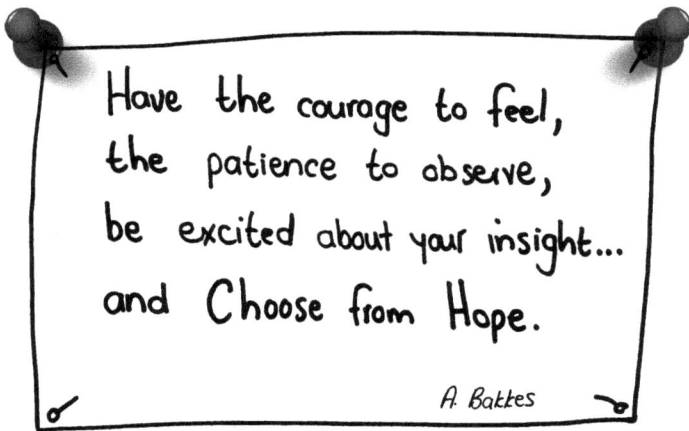

> Have the courage to feel,
> the patience to observe,
> be excited about your insight...
> and Choose from Hope.
>
> A. Bakkes

Being aware of our inner and outer world, aligning it in the moment, feeling our negative feelings with curiosity and compassion to self ... We might ask this question to help us. What if only 2% of what I am feeling is the truth ... can I love that?

Exercise 4: How to practise mindful observation

Take time to reflect on a two-hour period in your day.

Purpose	• To practise mindful observation • To become aware of how mindful observation impacts decisions and thoughts.
Outcome	• Continuous practice of mindful observation • Increased insight due to observation • Increased possible choices due to increased awareness
What is in it for me?	• Alignment between observation and perception • The ability to have quality insight and thinking
Engage	• You are required to engage an open mind and curiosity and focus without interpretation during this exercise
Resources (you will require)	• Uninterrupted reflection time • Time to journal (10 min per day) • A pen, pencil, journal or electronic device to journal on

- **Journal your observed behaviour** when you are in "autopilot mode". (Again, please try and suspend judgement as much as possible and then mindfully observe the type of decision you have made while in this state.)

- Journal the **observed behavioural or thinking patterns** over a period of a week.

- "If acceptance, empathy and positive regard are the necessary and sufficient conditions for human growth ... what do I observe about my

  o thoughts
  o feelings
  o actions

4.3 Love

The principle of love used in this model is used with the intent of practical love in motion in the workplace and other. I am not referring to romantic love, I am referring to the unconditional positive regard we practise with people we meet, work and live with every day. I am referring to the love in motion that we practise every day by being the best human being we can be with the tools that we have in the place that we find ourselves at any time.

When I researched the word 'Love', most of the articles and material indicated that love is so vast, with such a variety of faces and behaviour, that it is near impossible to pin it down to one definition or description.

Again I found some element of "love made practical" with Carl Rogers and Brene Brown. Rogers indicates that a form of love is to truly confirm the other person's being and the fact that what we see is a person on a journey and all we see are snapshots of that journey. To truly confirm another person is to accept the whole potential of the other human being.

How does love allow us to embrace our anxiety?

Love is ... accepting the whole potential of the other person

Again we find ourselves at the element of awareness that leads to acceptance of what is. Is it possible to look at another person and become aware of their potential? In order to do this, we have to practise our own self-awareness to truly see the other person for what and where they are in their journey. The moment we invite the curiosity to "seek to see what is", it is nearly impossible to stay anxious. When we seek potential in other people rather than criticism (only a form of judgement to keep us safe and certain), or otherness, we find that the human connection has no substitute.

Remembering that there is no replacement for human connection

Human connection is the energy that is created between people when they feel seen, heard and valued; when they can give and receive without judgement.[42] Some people might break out in a cold sweat at this thought that we are hardwired for connection because that will require us to feel and be aware enough of ourselves and our environment in order to make a conscious decision to connect with people. Often we have the response of … what if they see me and see my flaws? These thoughts alone are enough to make us anxious, yet exactly the opposite happens if we invite courage and curiosity.

I recently had the opportunity to attend an Agile facilitation and coaching course with Lyssa Adkins (ICAgile). My role in the room was what they would call a journey lead … a person who sits in the back of the class, observes the training and processes in order to be able to train the material at a later stage. You will notice that the word "observe" comes up again. The whole session was one amazing gift on so many levels. We were 34 people in a room in Stockholm for five days with pretty intense material to observe and integrate. Very few people in the room had English as a first language and very few people came from the same country. So here we have it: 34 strangers, different languages, different nationalities and different jobs, and yet the human connection was the one thing everyone in the room understood. At the beginning of the week a training alliance was done in order to create some certainty around behaviour and outcome and this served as an exercise to create awareness and acceptance of what was to come in the next five days. When the last day came and people had to give their final input on their learning and experience, every single person gave feedback on the human connection that was formed and created and how it made them better people, better students and people with courage to implement what they had learned back at the place of work. Every person felt a sense of ease to be as connected as they could be in their journey of life. There was no anxiety in the room – quite a bit of discomfort, but no anxiety.

Creating a sense of ease

Another practical manifestation of love is creating ease for the person or people you are with. (We will learn later that we cannot think when we are afraid, so a sense of ease is imperative for quality choices.) Nancy Kline describes this ease as "a presence defined by an absence."[43] It is the absence of tension or rush that allows the human mind to broaden and reach for new ideas. Urgency keeps people from thinking clearly. A space of ease causes people to see a solution almost instantaneously due to the mind not being tangled up in a race to solve emergencies. Kline puts it as follows: "Ease creates. Urgency destroys."

In order to create a sense of ease around us, there has to be a form of being at ease with ourselves. Think about the people that you know who are really just comfortable in their skins. These people are not perfect, not without flaws and not always right, yet it is really easy to be around them and be ourselves due to the lack of judgement, the easy connection and the sense of ease that we experience. As I mentioned, an important ingredient in this potion is self-love.

Self-love

Throughout my life I have noticed how we have really taken the concept of self-love and turned it into many things it is not. Although narcissism, functional psychopathology and other disorders exist, they are sometimes mistaken for self-love. If we do not have a level of self-love it is not possible to display practical love to other people. And this is amplified when we are parents, leaders of teams and friends … so pretty much all of us. Human beings learn through a certain behaviour being modelled. A little example of that is a son who did not make the sports team which he had hoped to do. He was young, around eight years old, and he sobbed to his mom that he had failed because he did not make the team. His mother went to great lengths to explain to him that he was not a failure and that not making the team is part of getting to know life. After he listened carefully he apologised to his mom for crying. His mom was very surprised by the comment and asked: "My dear, why would you apologise for crying?

It is part of how we learn and express." And the boy answered: "But Mom, I have never seen you cry."

This is just one example of how we think we should be and thus model the behaviour that stems from the "judgement of Should", yet people want to see in others what they want to show the least ... vulnerability, openness, courage and many many more.

I have found that practising self-love needs awareness of what is, acceptance of who I am right now, compassion to see who I am and deep courage to live in a way that models the behaviour I want to see in others. Personally for me, this is work in progress every day and every day I am a little more of me and I am OK with the fact that I do not have it waxed.

Listening

Again Nancy Kline brings so much wisdom around love in the form of listening. I would like to ask you a few questions. (This ties into being present, so you might see the same thing more than once in the following pages.)

- How often are you in a work meeting and while the meeting is going on you are thinking of your previous meeting or your coming meeting/conversation?

- How often do you listen to someone with the intent to answer with a ready-made comment rather than really listening to what is being said?

- How often are you in a conversation with someone and thinking of other things you have to do or something else that is on your mind?

- How often are you in your family or friends' presence but busy with your own thoughts, battles and worries?

- How often do you forget what was said, double book meetings, miss appointments, forget the conversation you had or only remember bits and snippets of what was said?

Do I listen to answer
or
Do I listen to hear?

Based on N. Kline

When I do "Embracing Anxiety" workshops, we have a practise during the entire workshop where people form a "thinking partnership" (based on Nancy Kline's work).[44] And during the entire day people get to practise practical love through listening to hear. People are not allowed to interrupt each other and are asked to do level 2 listening (also known as deep listening) and really hear what the other person is saying on more than one level. Without fail the feedback around this goes: "I cannot believe that no-one interrupted me." "I felt awkward hearing my own voice without people saying something while I speak." "I cannot believe how loved I felt by someone listening only to me." "I really feel heard and that allows me to connect with the person in front of me."

This leads us to the next step in our recipe of "Love in motion". Being present.

Being present in the here and now and engaging with others in ways that are not distracted

Being present in someone else's presence is possibly the thing we find the hardest to do as human beings and interestingly enough when we are NOT present we are anxious because we are somewhere else, solving other problems and then having to catch up with the conversation we just missed out on because we were not there.

David Rock indicates that everything we do in life is based on the brain's determination to minimise danger and maximise reward. Being present with another person is one of the best ways to minimise anxiety because you are only there and nowhere else in terms of thought, feeling and most of all … focus. It is interesting that by not being present we increase uncertainty as well as complexity and thus our anxiety. It is a strong trait of the "autopilot" in us to hide behind being busy and thus not focus on where we are at the specific moment in time.

It is here that we need to start referring to choice. Being present with the person/people in front of you is a choice. This is a liberating thought as it gives us perceived control, yet the magic happens when we choose to be present and we learn that it enables us to trust ourselves and our decisions. It is very difficult to be anxious while in a space of trust. The opposite of control is not out of control … it is trust. Being present enables us to trust ourselves, our decisions and the relationship with the person in front of us. If we are really present we can see, hear and value the people in front of us.

The capacity to see and be seen; to hear and be heard. This ensures that there is a culture of truly valuing one another and being valued.

As a child myself and my siblings were raised in a belief system that went something like this: You must see others, but not be seen; you must listen to others but not take up too much airtime yourself. As for valuing other people … always, allowing ourselves to be valued … not as much.

You may have been raised differently and were possibly not even allowed to be seen, heard or valued, and now is the time to change that. Not being seen, heard or valued increases our anxiety exponentially and is deeply related to our fear of "not being good enough".

One of the elements of love in motion or practical love is to:

- See people. This ties in with our ability to suspend judgement, to observe and see people for who they are, as well as practising love. Do we see people for who they are or are we seeing our judgement? As we know, if we see them through our judgement our anxiety increases and our levels of being present decrease.

- Be seen: Do we love ourselves enough to allow people to really see us? Just see us? I find that when we live in judgement and not in love we cannot allow one of the things we want the most. Just for people to see us, acknowledge us and love us. Again this ties back to: Do we love ourselves enough to see ourselves and in turn allow people to see us and blossom?

  I observe my children and see how they absolutely love to be seen, to be actually seen and how it motivates them to be more of who they are. Of course there are some theatrics involved, but when you are seven and five years old, I would hope that it just is ... I learn a lot from my children and often wonder what it is that stops me from allowing people to really see me.

Another one of the elements of love in motion or practical love is to:

- Really hear people. This ties into being present and active listening as we have discussed. When we listen to hear, are present to observe and ensure that people know that they are truly being listened to, it is nearly impossible for either party to be anxious.

- The other part of that is to allow people to hear us. We often do not speak up due to our fear of being wrong, not right or being inappropriate, yet when we really allow people to hear us, to listen to us, we have the opportunity to add value, build dreams (professional and personal) and change the world one situation at a time by merely being true to who we are. (Living our true north ... discussed under belief systems.)

The ability to value other people and be valued in turn:

- Again we firstly look at the ability to value people for the skill and the energy that they bring. This takes us back to being aware enough to see what the other person has to offer even if it is a skill or an attribute that might not be fully utilised in their current role. As leaders we make a big impact when we can match the value and skill that a person offers with a role that requires that skill. In doing that we find an amazing match where people want to perform, want to contribute. When people know they are valued, they find it very difficult to be anxious because they can see their own value and life contribution.

- And then there is the challenge of allowing people to value us. I have found that we live in the tension of really wanting to be valued and pretending that we do not need to feel valued. Here it is again important to integrate our level of self-awareness to see what it is that stops us from allowing people to value us, OR that people do value us but not in a way that we can or want to see it.

- *An example* to illustrate how people behave and respond when they are heard and valued could be found in one of the companies I worked for. At a point in my career I headed up the infrastructure department of a South African retail chain. We went on a drive to show the staff that they were valued and we tried many incentive schemes and reward policies. After a few months we did not see the change we expected and only then did I sit down with the team to ask them: "What do you need in order to feel valued?" The answer was astonishingly simple: Fast and up-to-date equipment (laptops and multiple screens) and good coffee that they did not have to pay for. What a revelation!!! These highly technically specialised people wanted things that made them work more effectively and thus felt they could add more value and in turn feel valued. The team dynamics and productivity changed significantly and so did the team's gratitude for being heard.

Being able to speak the unspeakable in the interests of openness and honesty which enables all participants to address issues in ways that are constructive

"Unspeakable" seems like a difficult word to work around, yet it is more about having the really difficult and pivotal conversations in a constructive way. We all know how anxious we can be in anticipation of a difficult conversation. Often our anxiety is born out of the "lack of control" over the outcome of the conversation and our "attachment to the outcome" of the conversation. A practical way of love in motion is to start the conversation with the spoken intent to be constructive in our way of thinking and behaving. The moment you enter a conversation, meeting, relationship and situation with the spoken intent to be constructive it changes the entire flow of the conversation in a positive way. It allows the participants to feel less judged and thus, less anxious, and the actual process and action of interaction then leads to connection. The conversation might still be uncomfortable but the actual charge and tension is significantly less due to our open spoken intent to be constructive.

Valuing "different truths" and acknowledging that even when one is in total disagreement with others, it is necessary to explore and find the "2% truth" that lies within the perspective of the other.

There are many schools of thought that support this way of thinking, arbitration and conflict resolution. For the purpose of embracing our anxiety, it helps us to reduce the complexity and uncertainty when we realise that there is some form of common ground when we are interacting with another person. This way of representing love is particularly helpful in family, small businesses and diversity contexts. When there is the possibility of 2% understanding of each other's point of view, a 2% common truth, it sets the scene for what could be possible.

Finally I agree with Christo Nel[45] when he quotes Koestenbaum and Kierkegaard[46] when he says: "Love without anxiety is denial of reality." What I would like to add to that is that love is far tougher, far more compassionate and far more courageous than we live it. It is possible to love in such a way that you and the person/people with you can experience anxiety as normal and not scary but a very real way of living and loving.

Summary: Practising Love is …

- Accepting the whole potential of the other person

- Remembering that there is no replacement for human connection

- Creating a sense of ease

- Self-love

- Deep listening

- The capacity to see and be seen; to hear and be heard. This ensures that there is a culture of truly valuing one another and being valued.

- Being able to speak the unspeakable in the interests of openness and honesty which enables all participants to address issues in ways that are constructive.

- Valuing "different truths" and acknowledging that even when one is in total disagreement with others, it is necessary to explore and find the "2% truth" that lies within the perspective of the other.

4.4. Gratitude

"True happiness is to enjoy the present, without anxious dependence upon the future, not to amuse ourselves with either hopes or fears but to rest satisfied with what we have, which is sufficient, for he that is so wants nothing. The greatest blessings of mankind are within us and within our reach. A wise man is content with his lot, whatever it may be, without wishing for what he has not."[47]

"Embracing Anxiety: Coming back with HOPE." It is within practising gratitude that one finds the practical opportunity to come back to whatever it is that you are facing with a sense of hope. (As we have said earlier: Coming back with hope = Resilience.)

My experience with gratitude is that it breeds creativity and serves as the foundation for powerful thinking and decision making. We are still going to look into choice and when we make our decisions from a place of gratitude the side effects are terrific. Steve Maraboli has the following saying: "Sometimes life knocks you on your ass ... get up, get up, get up!!! Happiness is not the absence of problems; it's the ability to deal with them."[48] I would like to take this quote and change it a little. Happiness is when you deal with your problems in an effective and soulful way, gratitude is embracing those problems and changing them into possibilities and at the very least life-lasting lessons that we apply every day in the wisdom of our behaviour. So to add to Maraboli: Sometimes life whispers, sometimes life shouts and then it kicks you up the ass. I hope with all of my heart that reading this book helps you to listen to the whispers long before the kick comes around.

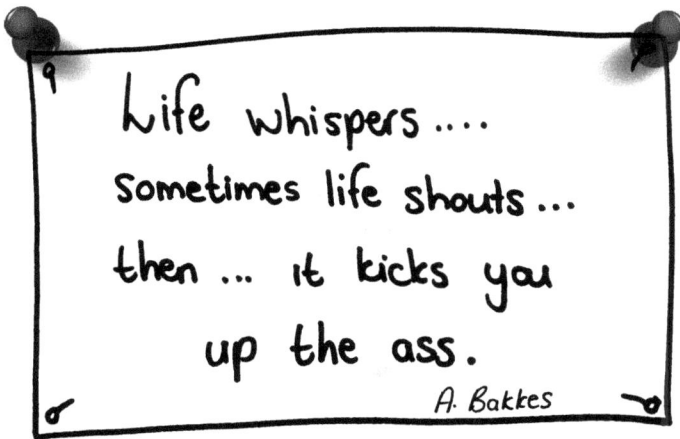

Life whispers ....
Sometimes life shouts ...
then ... it kicks you
up the ass.
A. Bakkes

I would like to look at practising gratitude in four areas of our lives, these areas being: Personality & Social, Emotional, Career and Health.

Personality & Social

Grateful individuals report higher levels of life satisfaction and optimism and greater energy and connections with other people. Grateful people enjoying these types of positive outcomes from their acts of gratitude would seem to make for productive and happy people. Gratitude generates what we call social capital. When we actively practise gratitude it causes us to be more trusting of self and others (refer back to our section on Love). Gratitude also makes us nicer, more appreciative and easier to be around. When we are grateful we tend to be like magnets for other grateful people and this enables us to create meaningful networks (work and other) as well as starting to appreciate the relationships that we have. As a result of gratitude all our relationships increase in meaning and depth. This includes romantic relationships, friendships as well as the relationship with our children. In the case of the relationship with our children, we model behaviour that empowers our children to do the same. When we model the behaviour of practising gratitude we have the ability to influence our friends, family and close relationships to be able to listen to the whispers of life and make their decisions from gratitude rather than desperation.

Emotional

Gratitude reduces feelings of envy, makes our memories happier, lets us experience good feelings, and helps us bounce back from stress. Gratitude enables us to grow and not merely change. Research has shown that gratitude enables us to go from PTSD (Post Traumatic Stress Disorder) to Post Traumatic Growth. These two expressions of living are vastly different and again are tied into choice. When the traumatic elements of life come our way and we practise gratitude, we are able to grow from the experience and go less into the stress and anxiety of the experience. This alone has the ability to change the entire way we engage with life from "anxious" to "worthy".

Gratitude reduces a multitude of toxic emotions, ranging from envy and resentment to frustration and regret.[49] Robert A. Emmons, Ph.D confirms that gratitude effectively increases happiness and reduces depression. Practising gratitude makes us feel good, increases our willingness to be open to positivity and enables us to live with happiness and joy.[50]

Career

Grateful behaviour can facilitate many positive interpersonal and community relationships that may in turn influence other key outcomes. Effectively applied in the workplace, for instance, gratitude may positively impact such factors as job satisfaction, loyalty and citizenship behaviour, while reducing employee turnover and increasing organisational profitability and productivity. In addition to the external benefits of gratitude accruing to recipients and their organisations, research surrounding gratitude identifies several positive impacts that await individuals who express gratitude to others. In turn, these personal benefits may also work to the advantage of organisations.

Gratitude enables us to be better leaders and managers due to the fact that we are prepared to acknowledge and be grateful to the people who assist us in daily tasks and achievement and to actively model gratitude towards the people we work with. People respect gratitude in others and it motivates us to do more and be more. Furthermore gratitude enables us to grow our network and increase our goal achievement. Results have shown that people who keep gratitude journals had a higher percentage of goal achievement than people who did not practise gratitude.

It is important to note that gratitude improves our decision making due to the fact that we have the ability to choose from a healthy perspective, a growth mindset and not from desperation. We will address decision making at length. Finally on the career front, gratitude increases our productivity because we are not spending our mental and physical energy on constant worry, fear and focusing on problems that cannot be solved due to our judgement of the past. (Remember "should" vs "next time".)

Health

Grateful people experience fewer aches and pains than other people and throughout all the research it is shown that people who practise gratitude are also more inclined to take care of their health. People who practise gratitude exercise more often and are more likely to go for their regular check-ups. For many years research has shown that not only does gratitude reduce stress but it plays a major role in overcoming trauma. Furthermore, grateful people tend to be more optimistic, a characteristic that boosts our immune system.

On a more personal front for me, the research indicates that people who expressed hope and practised gratitude during cancer diagnoses and treatment lived longer and did not relapse. The only common denominator between these patients was their shift towards hope and a positive attitude.[51] When Norman Cousins (UCLA Medical School) surveyed oncologists around important psychological factors in fighting cancer more than 90% of the physicians said that attitudes of hope and optimism (gratitude) were what allowed their patients to live longer and have less re-occurrences. In addition to gratitude the physicians indicated that a fighting spirit, a strong will to live and a sense of humour are some of the other common factors that help cancer patients to survive and stay healthy.

Now, if these elements of gratitude help cancer patients heal, survive and stay healthy the same elements must go a long long way in helping us cope with out anxiety during the times when life whispers and shouts.

Table 4.1: The positive side-effects of gratitude

Personality	Emotional
• Less materialistic (because our relationships increase in meaning and depth) • Less self-centred due to increased interest in our deeper relationships • More optimistic due to the increased awareness of what there is to be grateful for • Increases self-esteem due to increased levels of self-trust, trust of others, and increased appreciation of what is	• Helps us come back with hope through substituting post traumatic stress with post traumatic growth • Increases good feelings due to our change of focus and awareness • More relaxed due to changed perspective on life • Increases our resilience because we understand the essence of HOPE • Reduces feelings of envy due to higher self-esteem and chosen growth • Gratitude increases our sense of humour
Career	**Health**
• Improves our management and leadership by acknowledging people on our journey for their contribution • Increases networking by valuing our relationships • Increases goal achievement though practising gratitude for what we have already achieved as a motivator to achieve more • Results in improved decision making • Leads to higher productivity	• Increased sleep due to being more relaxed and better quality of sleep • Less sick due to stronger immune system • Increases longevity due to regular check-ups and regular exercise • More available energy because our bodies are not using our energy to fight. • Strengthened immune systems and general health due to practising gratitude • Increased health due to practising optimism and maintaining a sense of humour. When our body does not have to use the energy it has to fight but to live, we live long and healthy lives

Source: Happierhuman.com (Sept 2015) Amended by A. Bakkes [52]

What gratitude is NOT:

Relief: We often mistake gratitude for relief. According to dictionary.com relief is when there is an alleviation, ease or deliverance through the removal of pain, distress and/or oppression. Relief is when pain, distress or anxiety is removed or taken away.[53] The difference between gratitude and relief is that we can be grateful in the midst of some pain and discomfort. Relief is the "absence of" and gratitude is "in spite of".

Indebtedness: Gratitude is not the same thing as indebtedness. Indebtedness is a negative emotion which carries an assumption of repayment. Gratitude is not the same thing as weakness. Gratitude is the acknowledgment of kindness with thanks and no expectation of repayment of any kind. Often when deep gratitude is practised, the thought of anything in return does not even enter the space of the person who is being grateful.

✏️ Exercise 5: How to practise gratitude

Purpose	• To practise gratitude • To become aware of how practising gratitude changes your thoughts, actions and environment
Outcome	• Knowing what you are grateful for • Wanting what you already have • Shared gratitude
What is in it for me?	• The opportunity to practise gratitude and receive the benefits • Long-term increased health and wellness
Engage	• You are required to engage your will and some discipline and focus without interpretation during this exercise • Engage one other person every day based on the instructions
Resources (you will require)	• Uninterrupted reflection time • Time to journal (15 min per day) • A pen, pencil, journal or electronic device to journal on

---

Three steps to practise gratitude (designed by C.D. Kerns[54] and adapted by A. Bakkes)

Short version:

1. Reflect on three good things every day.

2. Want what you already have

3. Communicate your gratitude.

So what does this actually mean? Let's see.

Reflect on three good things:

Take a few minutes every day to reflect on the day. Identify three things that happened during the day that you are truly grateful for (i.e. the robot turned green when you were late for a meeting, the honest and loving feedback from a friend, the love and support of your family). It is important to remember that there is no "right" or "wrong"; it purely needs to be something that you are truly grateful for. Write these things in a journal, make a mental note or type them on your smart device. This daily gratitude exercise has been found to increase your happiness and health.

Want what you already have

Kerns gives us a four-step approach to appreciate more of what we have, rather than constantly longing for the things that are absent, or that we do not have.

- **Step 1:** Identify the non-grateful thoughts you have, or the thoughts that focus on what is absent in your life (i.e. Why did cancer happen to me, if I was only more clever, it was unfair that he/she got promoted and I did not).

- **Step 2:** Formulate grateful and self-loving thoughts that will focus on the current good and change the self-talk that ignites new brain patterns (i.e. In the face of cancer I see growth and love around me, I accept my current state of intelligence and choose to learn and grow, I have job that enables me to choose if I want to grow or change).

- **Step 3:** Replace the limiting thought in step 1 with the liberating thought in step 2 daily in order to change our neural pathways and allow for the feel-good hormones to enter our bodies and thoughts.

- **Step 4:** Transform your inner decision to be grateful into outward action (i.e. what can I do for cancer not to own me, apply my current knowledge to better myself, be the very best in my current job to enable growth, transfer and/or a new job).

Communicate gratitude

Reflecting on your current situation and chosen gratitude, choose a person/s to share these choices and emotions with. Be specific in the gratitude that you share and be authentic and truthful about it. This changes the state of your brain to see opportunities rather than limitations. Practising deep gratitude strengthens our immune system as well as our cardiovascular system.

A few real-life examples to support what the research has shown:

Fake it till you make it: I recall the first time I was diagnosed vividly and wish this upon no-one yet I know my diagnosis is another person's divorce, death and/or other life-changing event. I remember that I drove home, I phoned my sister in Germany and then headed home to tell my husband. I had no idea what I was going to say. My husband immediately took on the role of the "warrior supporter" (a book on its own) and then the big question ... now what? I really resonate with so much of the research. My will to live kicked in immediately. I put laminated posters with words in my handwriting all over the places that I had to look at daily: my bathroom mirror, fridge door, the dashboard of my car and these posters (varying in size) read: **Love, Hope, Grace, I want to live.** A few weeks later I added **trust.** Ironically, I remember that somewhere in my teenage years my Dad told me "sometimes, my dear, love is an act of will". Never did I think that self-love fell into that category as well. I have shared most of my journey in the first chapter but it is safe to say that practising gratitude daily (without having this research at hand at the time) is definitely one of the things that contributed to my healing and survival. As I mentioned, I came to realise that for me grace is the ability to have free will to choose. Throughout my journey these posters and post-its were with me in some shape and form. As I progressed these "mantras" stayed with me and today they are gentle reminders on my bedroom wall that still read "love, trust and hope". There were times that I just did not have it in me to believe this without reminders and yet as I think back ... I did believe it.

So it does not have to be cancer, because we all have our own mountains but sometimes we all need to "fake it till we make it" because that is OK.

Figure 4.1: An example of personal affirmations or mantras

Short indication of a long life: A few weeks ago I gave a talk on "anxiety in the workplace" and the focus was on gratitude and how it changed our health in the workplace. In the audience was a lady who put up her hand when we did some group sharing and her story goes something like this. In the household that she was raised in, gratitude was part of the everyday way of being. The children were taught from an early age that gratitude is part of a daily way of being, not just a daily way of thinking. Gratitude was part of their daily conversations and as common as saying good morning and good night. Currently her parents are aged 93 and 95 respectively, they live in their own home, they are independent, look after themselves, are in good health and run their household without any help. It is possible that good genes and other factors play a role in their life, yet it was really amazing to hear this real-life story of possibility and the conscious choice this couple makes to show up every day.

My tyre burst on my way to a gratitude talk: Last weekend (Oct 2016) I was given material for a talk and for the book in a really interesting way. I was scheduled to give a talk at a charity cancer event (being Breast Cancer Month) and I had to drive 110 km to get to my destination to be at the talk at 10.00 am. I planned my time and left 1 hour and 30 minutes before the event was due to start. About 45 km into the ride my left front tyre burst. It was with a little jolt of fear that I managed to stay in control of the car and pull over to the side of the road. Trying to practise what I preach, I started to breathe, acknowledged my shock and fear, and then started to think. I am no stranger to changing a tyre but I really have not done it for a good few years and I was truly "all dressed up with nowhere to go".

I got out of the car, took the spare tyre out of the boot and started assessing my options. At the same time a gentleman with silver-grey hair stopped a few metres in front of my car. He wore a khaki top and pants and looked at me and said, "Miss, you seem to be in a spot of bother. Let me help you." And that was exactly what he did – helped me. As he took up a position on one side of the hard gravel to see where to put the jack, I noticed a revolver in a holster attached to his belt. It looked like a pretty serious calibre, but not being a "gun expert" I would not really know. This gentleman changed my tyre, helped me put the damaged tyre back in the boot and made sure that all was good to go. As I offered my true and deep gratitude he insisted on driving behind me (seeing that I could only travel at 80 km per hour with the spare wheel) until I reached my destination. "Just to make sure you are safe," he said. And there I was, travelling to my destination with an angel "on my shoulder".

So how does this tie into practising gratitude? Let's practise: (Refer to steps 1 - 3 earlier in the chapter)

1. Be grateful: I was truly and deeply grateful that:

   a. I was completely unhurt.

   b. I was of the state of mind that I could clearly think about what to do next.

   c. a person had stopped to help me and that he had only positive regard for me and the situation I found myself in.

2. Want what I already have:

   a. I was raised by a father who taught me how to change a tyre and be self-sufficient in most things. This really helped me not to be anxious in the situation ... want what I already have.

b. The three of us (we are three sisters) were also raised with fierce independence and this helped me not to be freaked out by what happened. (I still had a fright, but I was not frightened) ... want what I already have.

c. I was raised around guns and hunting (not that I have hunted for many many years) and thus I was not intimidated by the gentleman's firearm at all ... want what I already have.

d. Lastly, it was surely going to cost me a significant amount of money to replace the two front tyres and yet I would be able to pay all my bills and still have enough to go out for dinner that evening ... want what I already have.

3. Share your gratitude:

a. And there I had a whole audience to share my gratitude with during the talk. I shared my experience and it made it all the more real and the people who attended the tea shared in my gratitude, went home and shared their gratitude with their "audience". All in all ... a pretty good day.

Finally: The "small" piece of information on a "long" bus ride:
Recently I went to Stockholm for a course and flew via Dubai. The plane stopped a few kilometres from the airport terminal. We took the bus to the main terminal building and it felt as if we were driving all the way back to Cape Town. While I was swaying in the bus, trying to keep my balance, I bumped into the gentleman next to me. I apologised and we started a conversation. It turns out that this person is a professor in oncology who specialises in colon cancer. When I asked his opinion of the role of gratitude in cancer survival he surprised me by saying something similar to this: "If my patients do not have to use energy to fight fear and pessimism, they can use that energy to be positive and fight cancer. It is a sure way to increase their chances of recovery."

I conclude this section with this: If practising gratitude can do so much for cancer patients, how much more will it not aid us when we are healthy, willing to grow and able to live happier and healthier lives through gratitude.

CHAPTER 5

The Five Steps of Embracing Anxiety

As adults, how do we learn a new skill in life?

When we approach embracing our anxiety as a new skill to be acquired, it is important to understand how adults learn (and grow if we choose to) and what elements are involved in these stages of learning in order for us to recognise them when they are presented in our learning (growing) curve. We often view growing and learning as a mental skill only, yet the heart and body are as important and impacted during our process of growth. We are going to look at the various phases in our learning process as well as how they impact our thoughts, emotions and bodies in the process. In anticipation of the growth we go through when we apply the Embracing Anxiety Model, it is useful to be able to identify in which phase we are and how that impacts our learning. The four stages of learning are described as follows:

Description of each phase of learning:

In order to illustrate the stages I am going to use two different examples in order to make it more real.

> **Example 1** is of a person that who has musical talent, already plays the piano and is consciously going to learn how to play a

new instrument: the guitar. In this example there is an existing understanding of the level of musical talent, the current ability and proficiency in playing the piano and the experience of what it takes to practise in order to be good or even excellent at the current skill – playing the piano.

Example 2 is that of a child who is learning how to ride a bicycle. In their current frame of reference they may not even be aware that they do not possess this skill. The child may or may not be seeking to learn the new skill and they have no similar frame of reference around this skill.

Stage 1: Unconscious incompetence/Novice

The individual does not understand or know how to do something and does not necessarily recognise the deficit. It is the place where **we don't know that we don't know**. When embarking on the acquiring of a new skill, it is often exciting because we don't know what we don't know. Some people may deny the usefulness of the skill and other people might just be too scared to obtain a new skill. The first step in acquiring the new skill is that the individual must recognise their own incompetence, and the value of the new skill, before moving on to the next stage. It is here where the awareness kicks in and allows us to see the current state of "what is". The length of time an individual spends in this stage depends on the strength of the need and the willingness to learn.

Example 1: The person is aware of the fact they cannot play the guitar yet very consciously competent that they are an accomplished pianist. In anticipation of the learning there is excitement and some underlying assumptions of "how difficult or how easy" learning the guitar will be. When we learn a new skill it is important to invite the enthusiasm and curiosity of what is to come.

Example 2: The child becomes aware that they do not have the skill in various ways. They might get a bicycle for Christmas or their birthday but do not know how to ride it. There might be a friend in the neighbourhood with a bicycle and that is how the awareness came to mind or there might be an older sibling who already has a bicycle and that is how the awareness was triggered. Based on various elements like personality, level of adventure and other internal factors, the child might have an assumption of how easy acquiring the new skill could be, yet they have no prior reference or experience.

Stage 2: Conscious incompetence/The Apprentice

Though the individual does not understand or know how to do something, he or she does recognise the deficit, as well as the value of a new skill in addressing the deficit. It is here that the realisation and increased awareness happens: **We know that we don't know.** The making of mistakes can be integral to the learning process at this stage. In this stage the **learners know they don't know.** This is that we realise that we are out of our comfort zone and the skill that we are learning might be more difficult than anticipated and not in line with our assumptions. It is also here that judgement kicks in (Why did I not know this earlier, I should have known how to do this, why did I not see this earlier). Due to the judgement we tend to give up during this stage of our learning. When we are learning a particularly tough life, emotional or spiritual lesson **we tend to get stuck here.** It is here that self-love, compassion and gratitude play a big role in getting us through this phase to the next phase. It is natural and normal to feel frustrated, doubtful and even anxious during this phase of growing. It is helpful to invite the mindset of discovery during this phase rather than judgement.

> **Example 1:** The person learning to play the guitar finds out that although both skills involve musical instruments, the technique to play, the sheet music and other elements of learning to play the guitar are nothing like playing the piano. It is easy to lose confidence during this phase, stop practising and just go back to playing the piano where it is comfortable and known. In order not to get stuck it is important to remember that this new skill

does not define us and it is a stage that we need to go through to get to the next stage.

Example 2: In the scenario where the child is learning how to ride a bicycle, this stage presents itself with many challenges of which some are: realising that their balance is of a certain nature and how to continuously correct in order to stay on top of the bicycle; learning that falling off might be painful but part of the process; realising that if they do not get back onto the bicycle they will not master the new skill. The fact that there are now more things to consider than before like: balance, looking in the direction of the area that you want to ride towards, looking out for pedestrians or cars or other bicycles, and then still having to stay on top and go at the best speed for their current level of skill, means that it is easy to get overwhelmed, scared and ready to give up.

Stage 3: Conscious competence/Journeyman

The individual understands or knows how to do something. During this stage **we know that we know.** However, demonstrating the skill or knowledge requires concentration. It may be broken down into steps, and there is heavy conscious involvement in executing the new skill. With consistent practice and feedback different levels of success are achieved during this phase. During this part of growth there is less frustration yet still awareness of the level of attention and concentration that is required to practise the skill well or to the level that it is mastered at the given time. If the practice continues over a period of time it becomes less challenging and more rewarding as well as enjoyable. Patience, acknowledgement of growth and celebrating the smaller milestones are elements that help keep us motivated and ready to try again.

Example 1: It is during this phase that playing the guitar becomes slightly less foreign, difficult and requires less effort. There is still refinement and fine tuning happening during this phase yet the level of confidence in playing the guitar has increased. It is during this phase that there is evidence that practising improves the skill and that patience and some compassion allow the person to move towards playing the guitar with nearly no effort at all. Patience and practice will lead to mastery.

Example 2: During this phase the child will have more confidence to ride the bicycle and has learnt what to do to stay on top, manage a good speed, make sure to be alert for any other traffic on the road and compensate where required. There is an awareness that the skill has been obtained and practised regularly. The finer technical movements might be outstanding but the basics have been learned and applied on a regular basis. The child's confidence increases significantly and the excitement and adventure return to the experience.

Stage 4: Unconscious competence/The Master

The individual has had so much practice with a skill that it has become "second nature" and can be performed easily. In this **stage we don't know that we know.** It becomes effortless and we might even experience magical moments that are driven by intuitive creative thinking. As a result, the skill can be performed while executing another task. The individual may be able to teach it to others, depending upon how and when it was learned.

Example 1: In this phase playing the guitar is as comfortable as playing the piano and the person can switch from the one instrument to the other. It is possible to have a conversation while you play the guitar and the focus is not on the skill any more as it comes naturally and is quite intuitive. To get to this stage the discipline of practice and re-choosing to commit to the new skill has been exercised regularly and with conscious awareness.

Example 2: It is during this stage that the child can ride the bicycle without any effort whatsoever. The finer technical aspects have been mastered and they might even try new tricks because the actual skill of riding the bike has been mastered in such a way that it is effortless. The child is able to ride the bicycle, navigate traffic, chat to a friend while riding as well as be clear on the route that they are taking to get to their destination. During this phase, the focus is on all the other aspects because the skill has been mastered.

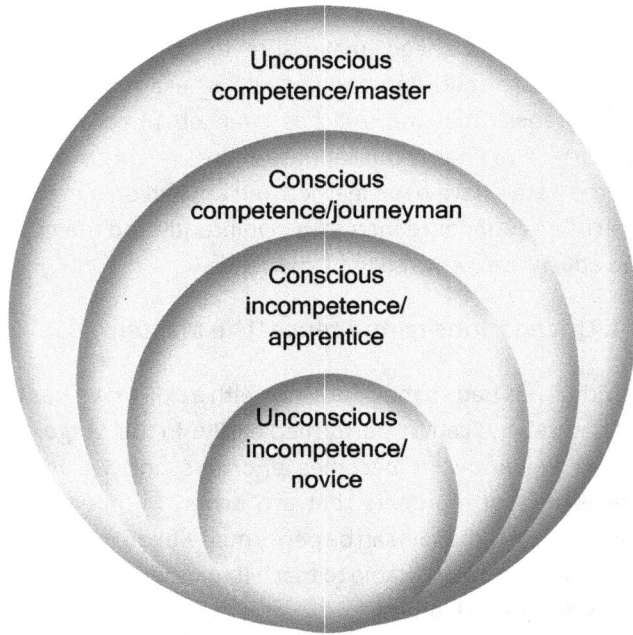

Figure 5.1: General phases of learning

5.1. Give it a name – identifying anxiety

In designing this model, I initially used the term "fear" as I did not completely understand the difference between stress, anxiety and fear. In my coaching practice I find that the words "fear" and "anxiety" are used to indicate the emotion that people experience and that impacts their emotions, thoughts and behaviour associated with the discomfort of fear or anxiety. In this model the word "fear" is used to indicate how the brain and body deal with our anxiety. To understand the differences and the relationship between stress, anxiety and fear the following explanations are given.

Stress: Stress is referred to as "the adverse reaction people have to excessive pressures or other types of demand placed on them". Additional to this we continue to define stress as "the harmful physical and emotional responses that occur when the requirements of a job do not match the capabilities, resources or needs of the worker".[55] Neenan and Palmer[56] indicate that the term "stress" is used in different ways depending on the person and the environment. In short, what the one person might find stressful might not be stressful the to next person. Our judgements, life experiences and awareness play a big role in what we perceive to be stressful or not. An additional way to think about stress includes the fact that it is a complex sequence of events that every person responds to differently due to the person's internal processes around the situation and/or the emotional reactions to certain situations, be they internal or external. **As an example:** One person might find entering a loud room full of people that they do not know a scary encounter that causes stress (or anxiety and fear), while for another person it might be an exciting encounter. The experience that is internal to the person's feelings and how the person perceives the environment add to how they react. We are truly all different and our reality is true to what we perceive.

Anxiety: When referring to anxiety, one view is that anxiety is "a vague unpleasant emotional state with qualities of apprehension, dread, distress, and uneasiness". How anxiety is differentiated from fear is that anxiety is objectless.[57] Another way to describe anxiety is "a feeling of worry, nervousness, or unease about something with an uncertain outcome."[58] In short, anxiety is this constant emotion that accompanies us and is often really difficult to describe and explain. The fact remains that it is experienced as ever-present and affects us in a negative way in the long term. Again, what causes anxiety in one person might cause no reaction or even excitement in another person. **As an example:** A trip overseas to a new unknown destination might cause great excitement and awaken a spirit of adventure in one person and in the next person it causes anxiety and fear. The fact that they might have to go to a place where they don't speak the language, might have to drive on the other side of the road and not know the ins and outs of the destination might cause them great anxiety.

Fear: When I was sick, the thing that caused me the most distress was the fact that I was afraid and anxious all the time and I was not sure about what to do with all these feelings. In researching fear it has been found that fear is seen as "similar to anxiety except that fear has a specific object".[59] Another definition of fear is "an unpleasant, often strong emotion caused by anticipation or awareness of danger and accompanied by increased autonomic activity."[60] An additional definition of fear is: "an emotion that is pre-programmed into all animals and people as an instinctual response to potential danger".[61] So in short it comes down to the fact that we feel fear when we feel in danger or, put differently, when we feel unsafe. Again it cannot be emphasised enough that fear is interpreted differently by different people. Different things make us feel unsafe or in perceived danger. **As an example:** When we look at the subject of public speaking, if you ask one person to speak in front of a group they might break out in a cold sweat due to the anxiety it causes them. The person next to them, however, might be completely comfortable to speak in public and sometimes on a topic that is not familiar to them.

We also have to note that to experience anxiety, stress or fear, there are times that it could be helpful and times that it is not helpful at all. It is reported that anxiety or tension is an essential survival signal of our body telling us that something is going wrong and we need to correct it. This mechanism serves to keep us safe and avoid potential danger in our day-to-day environments. Our built-in warning system is extremely helpful until it goes astray with exaggerated messages that cause fear for no apparent reason. I keep on mentioning that people react and experience things differently, yet no matter how different these may be, our perceived reality is the one we react to.[62]

If we remember that uncertainty has the potential to make us feel unsafe, it goes a long way towards understanding that we experience anxiety when we perceive danger. We are often faced with two different experiences – one defined in reality and one defined in perception (based on our belief systems). There is a true and accurate warning of danger that could exist – one that resides in reality and that we cannot do anything about as the situation cannot be changed (i.e. someone has had a heart attack or an accident has just occurred). This situation refers to healthy fear that could save our lives or cause us to take action that could be helpful to our situation. The other side of the behaviour that resides in our perception is when our built-in alarm system goes off but we do not know what is wrong and we feel out of control in the face of complexity or large amounts of uncertainty are present. This situation refers to our different perceptions, belief systems and way of being in the world that causes us to experience fear.[63]

In my search to find a way to deal with my anxiety in a practical and useful way I realised that I had to give it a name. The research supports this. According to the cognitive perspective, the most effective way to deal with anxiety is to **transform the anxiety into fear, thus giving the energy we are experiencing a name, making it certain.** This way we will know exactly what is bothering us and a plan can be devised to deal with what is feared.[64] When we label our emotions with a word or two it decreases the impact of the emotion in the moment. Labelling our fears and emotions is the key to staying calm under pressure and operating to the best of our ability. When we give our fear a name we engage the part of the brain that does goal-setting and when we set a goal, we believe that the end result is of value and worth working towards. In order for our brain to be able to take effective action, the brain needs to understand an idea. When looking at the Embracing Anxiety Model, this approach, to identify the true fear, is used to guide us. **Example:** In some people, the anxiety associated with public speaking causes them to literally start stumbling and stuttering at the very thought of it (feeling the anxiety). When we start looking at public speaking as a fear, we realise that the roots of reality and perception are intertwined. Some of my clients associate public speaking with the fear of exposure, the fear of public embarrassment and the like. Step one is just to become aware of the fear and observe it.

There is only one thing worse than knowing our fears ... not knowing them. Not looking at our anxiety is like walking around with spinach in your teeth the whole day. You wish you had looked in the mirror before you left. You would rather know about the spinach in your teeth than walk around all day without knowing. And yes, other people see our fears as clearly as they see the spinach.

Step 1: In essence we say: Take your anxiety and give it a name. Name your fear.

Exercise 1: How to give it a name

At this point we know that we have to invite our awareness and our observation and suspend our judgement to the extent that we can. The task at hand is to write down your three biggest fears and choose one that you are prepared to deal with in this process.

Purpose	•	To identify a fear that is related to our anxiety that we experience
Outcome	•	To become aware of our fears as they limit us and often drive our decisions and behaviour
What is in it for me?	•	We can only deal with our anxiety if we can become aware of how it translates into a fear. Our brain needs the aspect of certainty
Engage	•	Your courage to see what is there in terms of fear. Your feelings towards the aspects of life that cause you anxiety and the ability to observe the patterns of fear in your life
Resources (you will require)	•	A journal, uninterrupted time, mindful observation and honesty towards self

5.2. The belief systems that inform our fear[65]

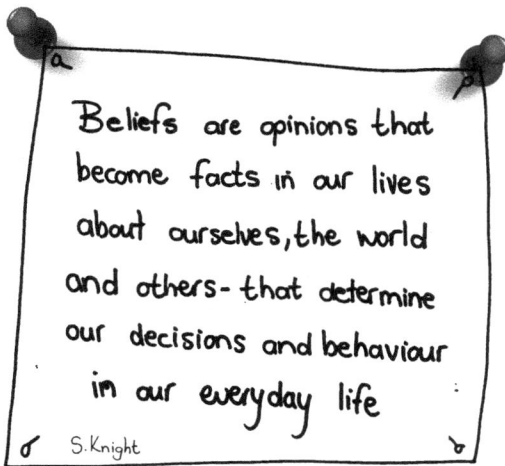

Beliefs are opinions that become facts in our lives about ourselves, the world and others - that determine our decisions and behaviour in our everyday life

S. Knight

When we start looking at our fears and anxiety in the light of our belief systems, there are numerous assumptions, life views and perceived ideas of how we think "the world should work" that we uncover. The research supports this thinking in the way that stress and anxiety from a cognitive perspective are due to the focus of the perceptions and the beliefs of the individual.[66]

When we think about our values and beliefs this is something that is understood by everyone but not always understood in the same way by everyone. Value is a concept that describes the beliefs of an individual or culture. Due to our diverse nature as human beings our references towards our values are completely subjective and informed by our childhood, the ways we were raised, the elements and people who made an impression on us during our lives. The thing about belief systems is that they are directly linked to the choices we make in life. Our belief systems guide our choices on many levels every single moment of the day.[67] Our belief systems are seen to guide our daily lives, the way we approach situations, how we think about them, how we feel about certain topics and, more importantly, our belief systems guide our decision making and our behaviour. When we become aware of the belief systems and values that drive our behaviour, we can also become aware of our fears and what values and belief systems inform our fears, and thus, our behaviour.

If we know this to be true, it is really helpful to question our current belief systems for truth and reality. As belief systems are based on assumptions, it is possible that those belief systems or assumptions could be beneficial or limiting to us. Nancy Kline teaches us that we make decisions based on assumptions that could limit our potential. Kline refers to the issues that prevent us from being our best as "blocks". "The blocks were almost always assumptions being made by the thinker unawares, assumptions that seemed like truth. These limiting assumptions [that people have] mak[e] it impossible for the thinker's ideas to flow further."[68] This takes us back to when we judge, the only thing we can see is our judgement. Our belief systems have the ability to keep us stuck and limit our growth. More often than not, these belief systems inform our fears.

The belief system has been cultivated in many organisations, cultures, friendships and society that an individual must manage their emotions or express emotions contrary to their true feelings. In some companies this even has a term; it is called "emotional labour".[69]

In my experience and in supporting research it is evident that our belief systems mould and influence our behaviour to the point that these belief systems become the scripts for how we live our lives. It is suggested that beliefs are opinions that become facts in our lives about ourselves, the world and others, that determine our decisions and our behaviours in everyday life. It has to be mentioned that this is the same for enabling and limiting belief systems. Enabling belief systems refer to belief systems that help us to perform and excel in life. Limiting belief systems are the belief systems that inhibit and limit our behaviour and our performance.[70] It is also important to remember that belief systems are not always formed by trauma or significant events. They can be formed by the way we perceive the world in the most subtle way or something we noticed in our life that caused us to build a certain belief system.

Another way of looking at belief systems via the lens of David Rock is that our belief system consists of our current assumptions of a situation or a problem that pushes out other possible solutions and answers due to these belief systems.[71] Again this links us back to our judgement at any given point in time. There are times that we think we know the problem so well that we cannot think of anything else. Belief systems that do not serve us lock us into a certain way of thinking that requires a new perspective. In order to have a new perspective we need to become aware of the current belief system. We often try to solve new problems with old belief systems and this often causes us to be stuck and link new experiences to old feelings.

It is important to note that we can change our belief systems. Some of our belief systems may have served us for a period of time, yet have now reached their sell-by date. Other belief systems will continue to serve and support us, and still others have never served us to start with. This takes us back again to become aware of the belief systems that support our fear, accept that we have them and then we can choose what action we want to take, if any.

> **Example 1:** I remember an occasion when I was a teenage girl round about 17 years of age. My sisters are three and four years younger than me and they were beautiful girls. (Today they are beautiful women.) I recall that I was standing next to one of my male friends on whom I had a crush, and we were watching a hockey game that both my sisters were playing in. The boy turned to me and said, "You must be the one with the personality." I was totally devastated as I interpreted his comment through my belief systems and what I heard was: "They are pretty, you are not." I recall how I have made so many decisions in my life based on that belief system that I borrowed from that young boy. For years I walked around with the idea that they are prettier than me. It took a lot of growing up and understanding of myself and my own fears to realise that all three of us have beauty and that we all look alike and yet so different. It is important to note that there was no trauma, no fear involved in the collection of this belief system. This boy's opinion was important to me and I took

it on as my own. An opinion that became my fact and informed many of my social decisions at some point in my life.

Example 2: When I started my Master's degree in coaching, I remember that I had a deep need to prove myself (a theme throughout my life). I was deeply motivated and at the same time had a strong fear of failure. I started off with the goal to complete my Master's degree in two years and obtain a distinction (mark above 80%). During the first year of my studies I fell pregnant with my daughter, had a full-time job and a toddler of eighteen months. As the year progressed I completed all the required studies and assignments. Emma (my daughter) was due in February 2011 and was born in November 2010. All of a sudden I had another premature baby and soon after realised that the cancer had returned in full stage IV. With all of this I decided to take a year off my studies and focus my time on my children and my health. I had many surgical procedures during that year in order to remove the cancer, my children were sick many many days and we spent quite a bit of our time in hospital that year for various reasons. I took up my studies again in 2012 and completed my thesis at the end of that year. So I seriously had to look at how my belief system of success served or limited me. I became aware that "success" in this case turned out to be something very different from what I thought it was. In the end, I completed my degree in three years, I obtained 65%, I survived cancer and was still raising two premature children (with the help of my loving husband). It suffices to say that I took my belief system around success and turned it on its head to become a supportive system rather than a limiting one.

It is in this step that we become aware of our belief systems and test them for truth and relevance and then choose to change them or not. In the following exercise we look at how. (We have the ability to change our brain and behavioural patterns. It is called neuroplasticity and is referred to later in the book.)

Step 2: Identify the belief system that supports your fear and choose to change it (or not)

Exercise 2: Change a limiting belief system into a liberating belief system

Purpose	• To become aware of our belief systems and how they impact our decisions positively or negatively. Limiting or liberating?
Outcome	• To be able to recognise some belief systems that inform your fear and thus enhance your level of anxiety on a day-to-day basis.
What is in it for me?	• To be able to see what belief systems inform your thoughts, decisions and behaviour. The possibility to change the way you think and engage with life through practising new belief systems that are liberating and that you can believe in.
Engage	• Your current awareness, courage to look at patterns in your life, a thinking partner that you can soundboard with – someone you trust.
Resources (you will require)	• Journal • Time – as much as you need. This process can take moments or days. • The ability to suspend judgement, observe what is there and the willingness to choose a new belief system where required.

Let's take the fear that you have chosen in the previous exercise. Write down the answers to the following questions with mindful observation and as little judgement as possible.

- What belief system informs this fear?

- What belief system do I subscribe to that supports this fear?

- Is this belief system true?

- If yes? If I accept this, what is possible? (remembering that acceptance is not equal to agreement)

- If no? What new belief system do I want to choose? Something I can believe in, even if it takes practice.

- In Table 5.1 are examples of fears and supportive belief systems: Please note that these are examples and they might resonate with you or you might have your own flavour of how it shows up in your life in a way that causes you anxiety.

Table 5.1: Examples of fears and supportive belief systems

Fear	Potential supportive limiting belief system
Fear of failure	Failure is weak Success defines me I have to be perfect in all that I do If I don't try I cannot fail
Fear of being seen as weak	I have to be unaffected by what happens to me. I have to be in control I have to contain at all cost I have to be "bullet-proof"
Fear of being seen as incompetent	Competent means no mistakes I have to know everything all the time Cannot show any form of weakness or "not knowing" Competent is being perfect
Fear of not being good enough	Only perfect is good enough Average is not an option Do it right or don't to it at all
Fear of not being perfect	I have to behave in a way that is appropriate in every situation I have to be right I have to get it right every time I have to prove that I am right/worthy/good enough

Fear	Potential supportive limiting belief system
Fear of not getting it right	I have to behave in the right way in any or most situations
	I have to get the information right
	I have to look the right way
	When I "get it right" I will be safe and/or will be accepted

5.3. The emotions, mind and body relating to fear

When we look at the Embracing Anxiety Model as a holistic model, it is imperative to invite information around how our brain works when we are anxious and how to help ourselves to use our brain consciously to lower our anxiety. The brain is very complex and for the purposes of our model we are going to refer to three major areas of the brain: the reptilian brain, the limbic brain and he neocortex. (This is referred to as the Triune brain by MacLean in the 1960s.)[72]

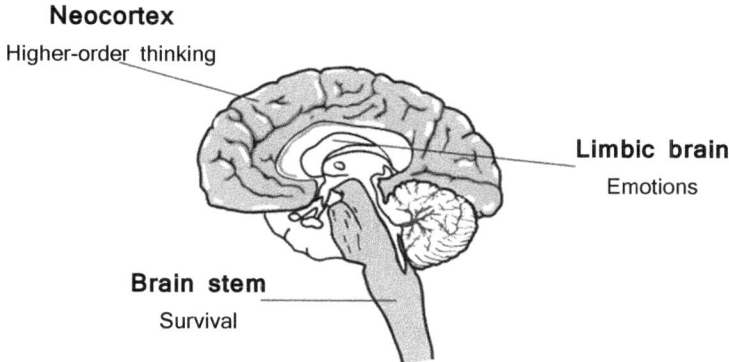

Neocortex
Higher-order thinking

Limbic brain
Emotions

Brain stem
Survival

Figure 5.2: Triune brain
Source: PageInsider, 2013[73]

The **reptilian brain** is the area of the brain that manages all the vital functions of the body. This includes breathing, heartbeat and balance. It is this part of the brain that helps us to survive in daily as well as extreme circumstances. It is here that our fight, flight or freeze responses to danger are generated as well as how we interpret that danger. This is the part of the brain that was developed first and as such was designed for survival in a relatively simple world (as opposed to the complex world we find ourselves in today). The **limbic system** (also referred to as the mammalian brain) is the centre where emotions are experienced and originate from and where feelings are shaped towards everything in the world that gives a person meaning. The limbic brain is also the place where decisions (and emotions) are managed in the human brain. As human beings we make countless judgements every day based on unconscious feelings and emotions and importance is assigned to every bit of information that the human being stores.[74] It is thus really helpful to know that every decision we make is linked to our feelings (even though we might think our decisions are rational, their origin is emotional). Due to the fact that emotions are managed in the limbic brain it is important to understand how the limbic brain reacts to fear and anxiety. The limbic brain is where patterns are formed and where relationships and feelings are mapped. The true power of this area of the brain resides in the fact it can make sense of itself and present the information together as a whole functional system that informs all our thinking. The challenge with having this information is that it helps us understand that we cannot numb our emotions selectively. Our emotions reside for the most part in one part of the brain and if we numb pain, hurt and fear we also numb joy, love and hope. We do not have the ability to numb our emotions selectively.

The neocortex (also called the cognitive brain or the thinking brain) is the part of the brain that gives us the ability to make sense of the world and where we create understanding.[75] It is also the part of the brain that is "responsible for the development of human language, abstract thought, imagination and consciousness" (Canadian Institute of Neurosciences, Mental Health and Addiction, 2012). Reflect on your thinking process rather than the content of your thoughts.

So why is this important? We cannot think when we are afraid and/ or anxious. If we think of what we have learned up to now there is amazing personal and theoretical evidence that can change our belief systems, thus change our fear, and as a result help us to become less anxious and embrace the emotions that come our way. Norman Doidge[76] teaches us that the brain has the ability to change itself and we call this "neuroplasticity". The brain actually has the ability to change it's structure through relevant exercises and activities. The brain can thus change in awareness and can change the emotions experienced.

Due to an increase in self-awareness and by practising acceptance and gratitude we actually have the ability to change how we think and choose new thoughts and experiences, and create new neural pathways that help us embrace our anxiety. It is important to understand how we deal with our emotions in this space, seeing that fear and anxiety are emotions.

Emotion

The following elements are classified as emotions. Sometimes we need to name them to express how we feel. Give your emotion a name.

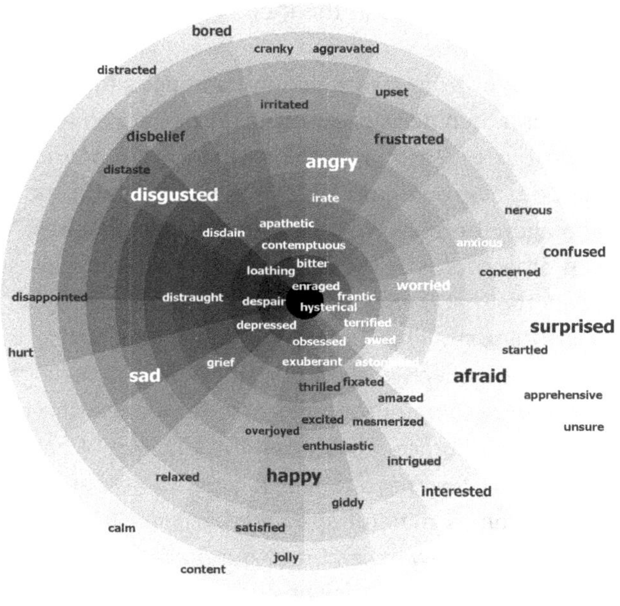

Figure 5.3: Emotions colour wheel
Source: Do2Learn[77]

Goleman tells us that fear forms part of the first five primary emotions and that these emotions are there for our survival. (Other emotions that Goleman cites are: Anger, Happiness, Love, Sadness, Disgust, Surprise.)[78] As we have discovered, as humans we have a deep need to feel emotionally safe and certain. We build many support and/or coping mechanisms throughout our lives and some of them are more helpful than others. The energy that comes from survival goes inwards to protect the individual; we tend to direct that energy inwards rather than share the emotions. Our emotions are automatic responses to what we perceive as danger and our ability to regulate our emotions, instead of being at the mercy of this, is central to being effective in a complex world. The ability to be aware of and to regulate our emotions is essential for thriving in life in general. When we can feel, we can live.

As we know by now, our decisions and our emotions are seated in the same area in the brain. It is therefore really important that we acknowledge our feelings when they arrive and to discover why they have presented themselves in the moment. The essence is this: To feel and to decide where our decisions are going to come from – from raw feeling or from aware mindful emotions that we translate into thought and then decisions. This takes us back to remembering to reflect on our process of thinking when the emotions present themselves to us. Strong emotion can create neural static or noise which sabotages the ability of the neocortex to maintain working memory. In other words, it is really hard to think in the presence of strong emotions. That is why when we are emotionally upset we say we "just can't think straight". Despite our intact intelligence, we make disastrous choices when we allow our emotions and feelings to own us. Goleman and others encourage us to harmonise the head and heart in order to embrace anxiety and live full lives. What does this mean? It means that we need to feel in order to heal and then make our decisions from a mindful space rather then from a wounded fearful place. This is how we embrace our anxiety, one decision at a time. The seemingly small decisions add up to good habits that add up to unconscious competence in making decisions with our heart and mind in an integrated space. How?

We go back to awareness. When we are aware of moods and feelings as we are having them, we can think about our thinking and start becoming aware of our belief systems and patterns of thinking and thus behaving. Mindfulness (observation and thinking about our thinking) helps us manage our emotions.[79]

When we are not aware of our feelings we often feel swamped by our emotions and helpless to escape them. It is then that our emotions own us and do not form a healthy part of us. (In that moment we feel that the emotion IS us and yet we are so much more.) This takes us back to accepting our feelings for what they are before we try and change them or choose from them. When we are aware of our feelings we tend to be accepting of our moods, and therefore don't try to change them from an unhealthy space.

Emotions that simmer beneath the threshold of awareness can have a powerful impact on how we perceive and react, even though we have no idea that they are at work. Once that reaction is brought into awareness we can evaluate things anew, decide to shrug off the feelings, consider them for what they are (remembering our belief systems, our judgements and the fact that we have a choice) and choose to change our engagement with the world in a way that is healthy and embracing of what is. In this way emotional self-awareness is the building block of the next fundamental of emotional intelligence: being able to choose what to do.

When fear triggers the emotional brain, part of the resulting anxiety fixates attention on the threat at hand, forcing the mind to obsess about how to handle it and ignore anything else for the time being. That is where the continuous feeling of anxiety comes from. We might even be busy with other tasks, conversations and/or other activities, yet the constant feeling of worry accompanies us. The worries could be stopped by shifting attention away. We do this through looking at out attachment, observing our pattern of thinking and inviting gratitude.

A few tips to change how you engage with your emotions:

- Become aware of your interpretation and the meaning you give to a situation based on your frame of mind (belief system). One of the things we can control and consciously decide is how we interpret a feeling, situation or event.

- Re-order your current information. All information in our brain is positioned relative to other information. Our information is categorised either as equal, less important or more important. There are times that we might have to re-order the importance of things in our brain in order to interact with the world in a different way. In our normal day-to-day lives we might call this letting go of a certain idea, getting over a certain thing or moving on from something. In all these cases we have used our brain's capacity to re-order the importance (attachment) to the information in such a way that we are less anxious or afraid.

- Being fixated on your own world view and not being able to see the world through another's eyes (linking to our judgement and our belief systems). When it is possible for us to look at a situation from a new position (vantage point) we can re-position the way we see things, and in this way it is possible to lower our anxiety. An example of this is to look at the same situation or feeling from another person's position, from your own position at another time. If we can practise this more often, it is easier to bring our anxiety levels down and to increase our ability to embrace what is in front of us.

Body

Our bodies are extremely helpful in telling us when things are out of balance or if we need to pay attention to certain areas in order to create the balance. It is interesting how many people just go into autopilot and override all the messages that their bodies give them. We pride ourselves on "pushing through" and "making it work" where our bodies are concerned. It is helpful to listen to our bodies, especially when we are avoiding our feelings and fears. Our bodies very quickly tell us when something is amiss.

Our bodies have an intelligence of their own and if we are prepared to tune into our bodies they are beautiful guides as to what is happening to us when our minds are too overwhelmed to see what is actually there. We all carry our stress in different places in our bodies. Here are some of the physical expressions of how we carry our anxiety, fear and stress. These are just examples, of which there are many more:

- Migraine: after a stressful period or a particularly stressful meeting or conversation

- Painful throat : A raw or painful throat. Sometimes this happens often and/or constantly if we do not express our feelings. The throat is the place where expression is situated (post-nasal drip included)

- Tight shoulders or knots in the shoulders or continuous neck pain

- Tight chest, chest cold, inability to breathe deeply, chest pains when breathing

- Tight ribcage or shortness of breath

- Tight or nauseous feeling in the area of the solar plexus

- IBS (irritable bowel syndrome)

- Restless legs

- Joint aches and pains

A healthy diet (consult a nutritionist or doctor), being active (anything from yoga to cycling) and monitoring how much we sleep and our alcohol intake are very practical things we can do in order to embrace our anxiety. When our bodies are supported, they can support us in turn.

Here are some ways in which our stress and anxiety and fear impact our bodies:

Table 5.2: Ways in which anxiety manifests in our lives

Some ways in which anxiety manifests in our lives	
COGNITIVE SYMPTOMS	**EMOTIONAL SYMPTOMS**
• **Memory problems**: Forgetting where you put the car keys, can't remember specifics of a conversation, or misplace things like important documentation, passport etc. before you travel or leave the hotel. • **Inability to concentrate:** We find our thoughts scattered, it's difficult to follow a topic in a conversation and to focus on demand takes a lot of energy. • **Poor spatial judgement:** We tend to misjudge our spatial environment. We walk into the corners of tables, nick our shoulders on doorknobs, misjudge the angle when turning a corner and scrape the wheels on our cars. • **Seeing only the negative:** In a conversation, work or personal context it is difficult to see the positive and we tend to focus on the negative and all the reasons why the idea or thing will not work. • **Anxious or racing thoughts:** We continue to focus on our anxious and worrying thoughts to the extent that we end up thinking of little else. • **Constant worrying:** We do not seem able to think of positive alternatives to any situation and we continue in a thinking pattern of worry and anxiety.	• **Moodiness:** We tend to be moody for no particular reason and only catch ourselves after the fact and not in the moment. Our moods tend to drive our behaviour. • **Irritability or short temper:** We tend to over-react, be irritable at small things and be short-tempered with day-to-day events. • **Agitation and inability to relax:** There seems to be a constant level of agitation present in the way we interact with the world. We do not seem to relax even if the situation is relaxing i.e. social situation, holiday, quiet afternoon. • **Feeling overwhelmed:** There is an underlying feeling of "just too much" that is our constant companion. It informs our thoughts, feelings and behaviour. • **Sense of loneliness and isolation:** It is possible to feel completely lonely in a crowd of people, at work and even with your close family. This is a tip that life is out of balance and you need to re-connect with self and others. Get professional help if you need to. • **Depression or general unhappiness:** We all have moments of feeling depressed and/or unhappy. When these feelings become more rather than less, get professional help.

PHYSICAL SYMPTOMS

- **Aches and pains:** Whatever aches and pains we have, stress, anxiety and fear enhance the ailment and it is amplified.

- **Diarrhoea or constipation:** The body tends to "hold on to" fluids when it is under stress and at other times there is so much adrenaline in the system that the body reacts to stress, anxiety and fear with diarrhoea. This is different for different people and even different for the same person in different situations.

- **Nausea, dizziness:** When we are in a constant state of worry and anxiety our body responds by causing a feeling of nausea in the pit of the stomach. Most of the time, this feeling does not provoke vomiting, yet is ever-present. The dizziness is similar to "getting up too quickly" and the world tends to spin without cause. In this case it is important to breathe down to the stomach for three to five breaths.

- **Chest pains, rapid heartbeat:** Due to constant worrying and fear, the body often responds with chest pains or rapid heartbeat that are similar to those experienced in a life-threatening situation and in some cases it signals the onset of a possible panic attack. Again, breathing deeply helps in this situation.

BEHAVIOURAL SYMPTOMS

- **Eating too much, eating too little:** Again this is different for different people and situations. Sometimes we cannot eat and other times we eat to fill the hole, thereby creating some certainty or comfort.

- **Sleeping too much, sleeping too little:** We tend to sleep too much, or at every opportunity we get. Sometimes we can spend an entire weekend sleeping and not feel refreshed on a Monday. The other side of the scenario is not sleeping enough. We either battle to fall asleep or we cannot stay asleep. We wake up at odd hours and cannot fall asleep again and the thoughts then seem to be around our anxiety and increase the feeling of concern.

- **Isolating yourself from others:** Some people react to the feeling of fear, overwhelmedness and other anxiety-related feelings by isolating themselves. If this is done for short periods of time it can be helpful, yet if this continues over a longer period of time it could lead to feelings of depression when we believe that we have to deal with all of what is happening to us alone and without help. This is not true. Sharing emotions is healthy and healing. Choose someone you trust or a professional.

PHYSICAL SYMPTOMS	BEHAVIOURAL SYMPTOMS
• **Loss of sex drive:** Clients often report a loss of sex drive during this constant state of worry, anxiety and concern. This is the body's way of indicating that it is using all the available energy to cope with the constant state of anxiety. This often has a negative impact on our relationships, self-esteem and confidence. • **Frequent colds:** During times of constant anxiety our immune system takes strain and we find ourselves in a situation that we "don't get over that cold". Our immune systems are negatively impacted by the constant anxiety and worry.	• **Procrastinating or neglecting responsibilities:** This is a very human reaction to feeling unsafe or anxious. We want to avoid and then we procrastinate and this is made worse as the guilt kicks in when we have not kept our promises or have not owned up to our responsibilities. The impact is negative on all levels. • **Using alcohol, cigarettes or drugs to relax.** This is one of the most common ways to avoid, numb the edges and hide from our emotions. The concern is that most types of alcohol and drugs leave us feeling worse once their effects have worn off and can lead to us feeling depressed. • **Increased nervous habits (i.e. nail biting, pacing, drumming fingers on tables, tapping feet).** Our bodies are extremely helpful. If the body wants to let go of the nervous energy it gives us cues. It is the body's way of telling us that something is out of balance.

When we look at the physical impact of anxiety on our bodies, there is an additional consideration as to how our behaviour (or suppression thereof) impacts us. Here are a few things to consider, referring to Figure 5.4 on page 108:

7.   What is our current relationship to what we believe in to trust and guide us through life?

6. How often do we listen to our intuition, our internal wisdom that we have gathered during our lives and do we listen and use our creativity or do we suppress it and ignore it?

5. Are you communicating your thoughts, needs and wants in life or are you avoiding communicating the things that are important to you?

4. What is your relationship with love? Do you give love practically and freely and more importantly, do you allow people to truly love you?

3. Do you stand in your power in a healthy way or do you give your power away?

2. Do you experience your emotions or do you suppress them?

1. Do you listen to your body and the signals it is giving you or do you continue until your body cannot continue any longer?

It will be helpful to keep this in mind as we start exploring how anxiety and fear impact our behaviour.

Main issue		Plexus/glands	Related functions

- Spirituality
- Relationship to
  God/TAO
- Universal source
	7
	TI
		Carotid plexus
		Pineal gland
			- Circadian
			  rhythms

- Intuition
- Wisdom
- Creative
  intelligence
	6
	LA
		C1-2
		- Carotid plexus
		- Pineal gland
		- Pituitary gland
			- Hormonal/
			  physiological
			  regulation

- Communication	5
	SO
		C3-7
		- Pharyngeal plexus
		- Thyroid/para-
		  thyroid plexus
			- Metabolism
			  and calcium
			  regulation

- Giving/receiving - Love	4 FA	T1-5 - Cardiac plexus - Heart/thymus	- Electromagnetic field generator - Blood pressure - Immune
- Personal power - Self will	3	T5-T9 - Solar plexus - Pancreas	- Digestion - Assimilation muscles
- Emotional balance - Sexuality - Procreation	2 REY	T9-L4 - Lumbar plexus - Sex organs - Adrenals	- Sexual functions - Elimination - Water regulation

- Survival
- Physical needs
- Tribal association
	1
	DO
		L5-S5
		- Lumbar and
		  coccygeal plexus
		- Adrenals
			- Adrenals
			- Fight/flight
			  response
			- Bones/skeletal
			  structure

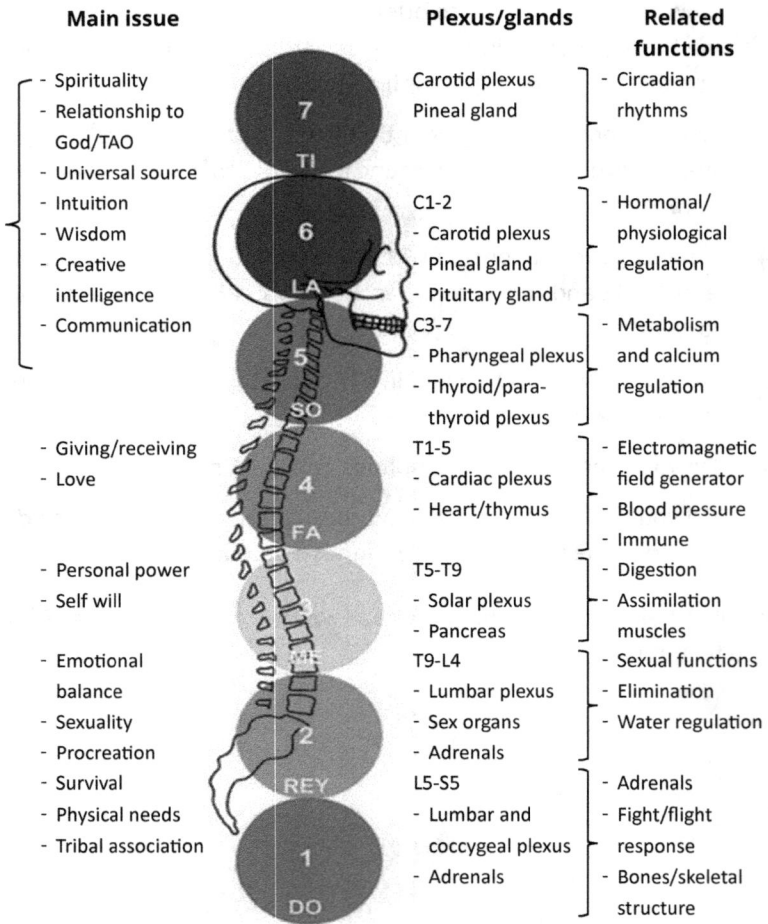

Figure 5.4: Self-healing tips

Source: http://www.paulcheksblog.com/chakra-balancing-made-easy/comment-page-1/

5.4. Our fear-driven behaviour

*"Stress causes one part of the brain to close down: It's the front part
of the brain ... responsible for the human capacity to integrate new
information, make complex decisions and creatively adapt ... So at the*

time that one most needs adaptive integration to find new ways to deal with the stressful event, the part of the brain that is able to undertake this task closes down – people become ineffective under stress because this important part of the brain stops functioning." [80]

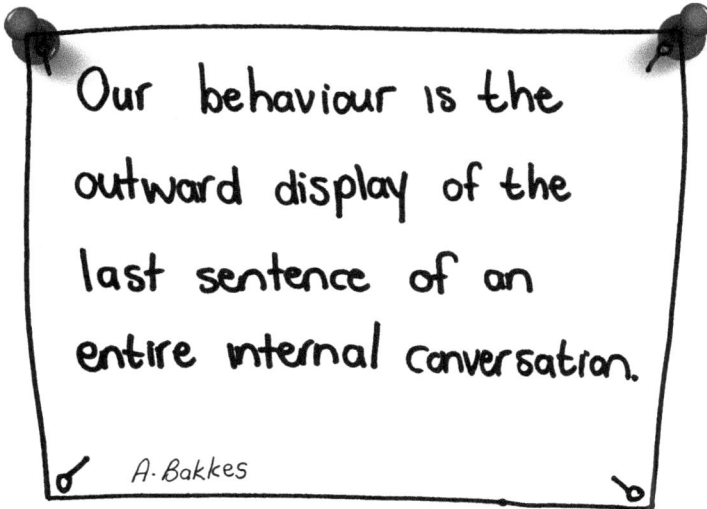

Our behaviour is the outward display of the last sentence of an entire internal conversation.

A. Bakkes

One of the contributing factors towards our behaviour when we are anxious is the ongoing process of truth management inside of us. Downs teaches us that truth management is when we deny ourselves the expression of the unique truth of who we are. As we learnt earlier, we measure our unique truth against assumptions and belief systems and then often behave in a way that we think we should based on our judgement and attachment to the situation. This truth about who we are, to the extent that we are aware of it, is often connected to powerful emotions that can cause a great deal of discomfort and anxiety when we translate it into behaviour. Or rather, the behaviour we think we should be presenting.

We know that our individual emotional states are what lie at the core of our individual attitudes and behaviour. When we remember that our decisions and our emotions reside in the same area in the brain, then we understand that our choice of behaviour is often based on the emotions we experience in that moment. The really interesting thing is that negative emotions and thinking impact negatively on our performance and work, as parents and in our lives in general. So when we are frustrated, angry and experiencing resentment we often do not express this truth of how we feel and then our behaviour is not true to who we are and we continue judging ourselves after the fact (Ashkanasy & Daus, 2002: 77). If all of the above is considered, it is safe to make the deduction that when we feel threatened, fearful or unsafe in any environment we do not perform at our optimal levels.

Again, the bottom line is that we need to feel a certain level of safety (certainty) in order for us to make our best behavioural choices. When we feel safe and secure we deliver a better quality of work (whatever that work might be) and we are more productive. In 1982 Deming did research on the performance of factory workers and what he found is true of all walks of life. When we do not feel secure, we cannot function at our best in anything we do, from parenting, loving, being a good friend, to our work and intimate relationships. The word "secure" is broken down as follows from its Latin roots: "se" which means "without" and "cure" which means "fear or care". "Secure" means without fear according to Deming. This indicates that people who feel secure seem to be without fear to express and enquire.[81] I found it so beautiful that our human behaviour could be captured in such a simple and powerful way.

We need to remember that we have storylines stored in our limbic system that are labelled as dangerous due to something we observed or that happened to us. The wonderful thing is we can now re-evaluate the truth and the appropriateness of those stories. Some of them might have reached their sell-by date and do not serve us any more. When we are over-stimulated and anxious the possibility of misinterpreting information and making connections to situations and/or feelings that are not true for that moment any more increases. When we are anxious all the attention goes inside and we do not observe the outside for reality. An example: One of my clients had to manage a team of people. She lead the team successfully and yet one person in the team caused her deep internal tension and she found that she behaved around him in a way that is not natural to her personality or leadership style. She was at a loss as to why this was. During coaching she discovered that this person in her team had exactly the same body language and mannerisms as her stepfather with whom she had had an abusive relationship. Deep in her fear memory these physical cues reminded her of danger and threat. Once she was aware of this she could re-programme her behaviour around this person. The discomfort was still there, but she chose to heal some of the old wounds and their relationship improved. She changed her behaviour.

So if we bring things together, if we can identify what we fear and what makes us anxious, we can review our belief system that supports this fear, and re-evaluate it for truth. We can use the signals our bodies and emotions give us to see when we are anxious and then we can behave in a way that we choose. When we remain anxious we stay trapped in our fears and we behave from our fears and not from our potential.

When we embrace our anxiety we enable ourselves to discover what the impact of stress, anxiety and fear is on our behaviour, and relying on brain plasticity and truly feeling our emotions, discover a way of changing our behaviour.

When we remember that everything we do in life is based on the brain's determination to minimise danger and maximise reward, it is useful to look at a few examples of how this could translate into our behaviour. Building on our fear examples, here are some behaviours we show when we are anxious. Remember that people only see the last sentence of your internal conversation through your behaviour. Remember that we all have different perceptions of fear and anxiety and we will behave in different ways towards different fears. These are examples of what I have seen, experienced, seen other people do and some research.

Table 5.3: How our fear translates into possible belief systems and related behaviour

Fear	Potential supportive limiting belief system	Potential behaviour we display
Fear of failure	• Failure is weak • Success defines me • I have to be perfect in all that I do • If I don't try I cannot fail	• I will over-compensate for what I perceive to be dangerous in order not to fail • I will do what I need to do in order to succeed even if it is at the cost of my own health, relationship or family in order to succeed • I will focus on detail that is not required for success in order to deliver the perfect product, presentation, book or piece of art • I avoid any situation, piece of work or relationship in order not to fail
Fear of being seen as weak	• I have to be unaffected by what happens to me • I have to be in control • I have to contain at all cost • I have to be "bullet-proof"	• I pretend to cope no matter what. I am always in a good mood, I "handle" difficult things in life as if I am unaffected and I "take it in my stride" • I control even the smallest detail of work of the people who work for me, my child's behaviour and/or my partner's decisions • I am in complete control of my life and I am never late, always organised, never "caught off guard" and my living space is always spotless • No-one will see how I feel. I will be blunt, short, defensive and insulting in order for people not to see my feelings • "You can throw anything at me, I will be fine." I will work long hours, I will stay up late, I will do what I need to do and you will not know how I feel inside

Fear	Potential supportive limiting belief system	Potential behaviour we display
Fear of being seen as incompetent	• Competent means no mistakes • I have to know everything all the time • Cannot show any form of weakness or "not knowing" • Competent is being perfect	• I use the need for more information as a way to prove that I am competent (worthy) • I am always right and my information is always right. I make no mistakes and if I do there is deep shame, defensiveness and blaming involved • I always have all the information required. I am an expert in parenting, my job, my field or work, sport, politics or all of the above • I always have the answer (and feel terrible if I don't)
Fear of not being good enough	• Only perfect is good enough • Average is not an option • Do it right or don't do it at all	• I will spend time to make something "perfect" long after the standard of what is required is achieved • My achievement, behaviour, parenting, friendship conduct and other behaviour (that I am attached to) have to be "above average" • I will always go the "extra mile" often at the cost of myself and my needs • I procrastinate on the things that make me feel uncomfortable, anxious, and fearful of the outcome and I rationalise why I find other things to do instead • I do things in a way that is not "exactly up to my own standard". Thus I prove to myself that I am not good enough

Fear	Potential supportive limiting belief system	Potential behaviour we display
Fear of not being perfect	• I have to behave in a way that is appropriate in every situation • I have to be right • I have to get it right every time • I have to prove that I am right/worthy/good enough	• We behave in a way that we believe is "right for the situation" based on our belief systems and fear of the other person's behaviour • Getting things right the first time (like a new spread sheet, presentation or any new skill) and when we do not there is deep judgement. (Ties into fear of being incompetent as well) • There is no room for error, so I expect myself to get it right without mistakes, do it every time (and make it look effortless) • When there a conversation, situation, argument, I have to be right and win the fight no matter the cost to feelings (my own and others). I will find the proof that I am right, or that I did what I said or that I can actually the task
Fear of not getting it right	• I have to behave in the right way in any or most situations • I have to get the information right • I have to look the right way • When I "get it right" I will be safe and/or will be accepted.	• I will change my behaviour in different situations, conversations and interactions in order to be perceived as "getting it right" in that moment. This may be in conflict with my internal truth • When I have a conversation my facts have to be exact and if they are not I will either not share them, or delay the answer until I have the "right" answer • I will not leave my house without the appropriate dress code or make-up. Wherever I go, I need to make the "right" impression • I will go to great lengths to get the answer, the behaviour, the dress code the party gift "right" in order to feel accepted and safe

It is important to note that some of these behaviours can be very useful at times. It is not always the behaviour that is the key, but where we choose to behave from. If we remember that our behaviour is only the last sentence that people see of the conversation in our heads, it brings us back to how aware we are of our thinking, our feelings and where we choose to behave from. Often the same outward behaviour can come from different places and the impact on self and the environment around us will be different.

Some examples:

Going on a diet: This is something most of us have tried. So we can buy the book, buy the relevant food according to the diet and then we have to actually follow the diet. When we choose to go on a diet because we do not like or accept our bodies and have shame and embarrassment about how we look, it is hard work, we feel deprived and we rarely keep off the weight. When we go on a diet because we love our bodies, want to put the best food into them and want to be in the best shape we can be, we approach the behaviour from a loving space. Then we are careful about what we eat because it is a self-loving activity. Both outward behaviours are those of "going on a diet" but the place we approach it from is very different and makes all the difference in the outcome. This takes us right back to how aware we are of our thoughts, feelings and bodies, and whether we can accept that we are where we are before we act. If we can, then the actions turn to achievement internally and externally.

Getting fit: Some of us have had this experience a few times in our lives. We decide to get fit (we will explore the core of the choice in a moment). Then we get the clothes, the running shoes, the mountain bike, the gym membership (or any other way you choose). And then we have to start our training. When we train from a place of: "I have to get fit because I have an ugly body OR I have to train because I have to achieve at all cost and prove myself to the world OR I have to train to stay thin and I cannot miss one session or one run OR it is the new cool thing to do in order to fit in and "get it right", our bodies do not respond well and we do internal and often physical damage. When we choose exactly the same outward behaviour from a loving and grateful place it looks completely different. Then we train because it is what our bodies need to be healthy. We do not over-train because we listen to our bodies. We get up early (not always easy) but we commit to ourselves from a loving space and not from a "not good enough" or "unhealthy drive" space.

As you can see, the outward behaviour might look the same, but the place we come from makes all the difference. We have spoken about behaviour from self to a situation and now we move to when we behave in certain ways around people and our relationships.

If we remember that our anxiety is fuelled by uncertainty and complexity it is useful to remember that our judgement and observation work for us rather than against us if we are mindful and aware. When we are in situations that feel emotionally unsafe, draining or overwhelming, the best thing to do is just become aware of how you are feeling. The awareness in itself changes the way we see the situation. We go back to our recipe:

Table 5.4: Practice part of our model: How do I behave?

Become aware of your feeling in the moment • Ask: What about this am I attached to? • What am I judging? • What belief system is playing out now?
Acknowledge the feeling internally: • I feel unsafe because I am new in the situation. • I am anxious because I am worried about what they will say, feel or how they will act. • I am afraid because he/she is shouting at me.
What are the possible ways I can react? • Expressive suppression: Pretend I am OK and push through. This often fails and backfires because due to suppression we explode at a time that is not relevant or worthy of the explosion and then we go back to judging ourselves. • Hold on to my belief systems for dear life and work very hard in the moment and become emotionally drained (long-term burnout).

> - Change the way I think about it through labelling my emotions or change the way I interpret the information.
> - Expression: Say how I feel in a non-threatening way and see what is possible from there.
>
> How do I behave and say what I feel? Here are our golden phrases:
> We give **impact feedback:**
> - When you ...... I feel......
> - When you ...... the impact on me is ......

Let's explore our golden phrases. This way of communication is called **impact feedback.** The people who promote non-violent communication bring this way of communicating and behaving as a gift. How does it work? Firstly you tell people what they do and this creates behavioural evidence. Then you tell them how it makes you feel and this is being true to who you are and the other person cannot make you "wrong" because your feelings are your feelings and there is no arguing with that. The second statement is very similar. You just give the person the impact they are having on you and again there is no arguing with the way you experience a situation. It is what it is. From here anything is possible and your anxiety will dissipate because you have acknowledged yourself in a productive and powerful way.

Some examples:

To give some context and explain our internal conversation versus our outward behaviour, I grew up in a household where we are three extroverted girls, my mom is outgoing and my dad was an introvert. We have strong opinions and we were encouraged to share them and have good conversations around the topics we feel passionate about. So we laughed and fought a lot around the dinner table. My husband grew up in a household of three introverted boys, an introverted mom and an outgoing dad. I often imagine them only talking to each other around the dinner table when they asked for the salt. So early on in our relationship and marriage we got to know each other as couples do ... through a few mishaps and re-calibrating. On one particular evening I felt very passionate about a topic and demanded that my husband have an opinion and these beautiful words left his mouth:

"When you speak to me like that it feels like machine-gun fire and I cannot think." As you can well imagine, the wind went right out of my sails. What on earth was there to argue about? He had just shared what impact I have on him and that was his reality. The first thing I wanted to do was change the way I spoke to him because I was not aware of how he experienced me. Now, after 12 years of marriage, we still do this with each other and it so much easier than wondering what is happening in the other person's mind.

Our best and long-lasting behavioural changes come from when we have "aha" moments that translate into insight into self and/or others.

5.5 How to change my behaviour: 5-step summary

Step 1: Become aware of how you behave when you are anxious and/or afraid. (Keep a diary over time in order to observe what the triggers and patterns are.)

Step 2: What in the situation do you judge and are you attached to?

Step 3: What belief systems do you have that support this fear and behaviour?

Step 4: Give impact feedback: When you...... I feel. OR When you....... the impact on me is......

Step 5: Choose: To give it a name, to label your emotions in order to express them. Listen to your body and the signals it gives you and choose to re-interpret the information at hand.

It is the 'small' consistent choices we make from Observation, Love and Gratitude that make anything possible...

You can choose to choose

A. Bokkes

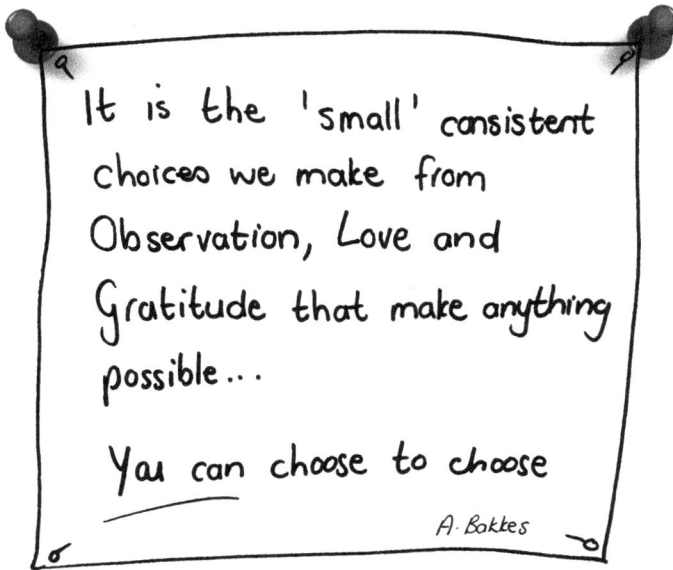

We go back to the beginning pages of our story and recipe. Are you aware that you can choose to choose? Are you aware of the current choices you make or choose not to make? It helps to remember that not choosing is also a choice. It is often not the choice. When we come back to our anxiety and fear, it is often the consequences of our choices that we fear, rather than the choice itself. And by now we know that when we choose from fear, these are not our best choices either in the short or long term.

When we take a step back from a situation and look at the bigger picture, then we allow our brain (right anterior temporal lobe) to connect the dots by pulling together distantly related information. By doing this, we allow ourselves to gain insight into the situation, feeling and/or company we work in. There is a strong correlation between gaining insight and the emotional state in the brain. When we are at ease, happy, content and grateful, it is easy to gain insight and make a holistic decision. When we are anxious, stressed and overwhelmed the likelihood of gaining insight is very little and our decisions are often knee-jerk reactions that we tend to regret or over-compensate for.

An easy way to look at our decision-making process is given to us by David Rock and it aligns with all that we have been saying up to now. It is called **ARIA:**[82]

> **A** – Awareness
>
> **R** – Reflection (or as we call it mindful observation)
>
> **I** – Insight
>
> **A** – Action

Let's try this example: While writing this book, my focus was on meeting my deadline and everything else I chose to treat as "Just In Time" and I communicated with my colleagues and clients only enough in order to stay professional and manage expectations. (Already a few flawed baseline assumptions here and limiting belief systems.) In doing so I double-booked two important workshops on the same day. My colleague sent me an e-mail where she enquired about the time as she saw both activities in the dairy. I felt guilty and immediately replied that my workshop had been in the diary for months and that it must be a mistake. She in turn replied that the other workshop had also been in the diary for months. Only then did I see the potential danger lights. OK, so what do I choose? I took a step back and looked at the bigger picture. I had been focusing on completing my book and other matters had been receiving less focused attention. We both have hectic schedules and she was trying to get us together. It was the end of the year, we were all tired and we all wanted what was best. I know my colleague and she is not the fighting, blaming type. She was merely trying to get us in one place for a period of time. It was then that I picked up the phone to get the ease and clarity back between us. After a five-minute conversation we were clear on what to do and I apologised for my contribution to the situation.

So what happened?

1. I came from a place of guilt and chose to send an e-mail that would prove my innocence in the matter. The fear of being wrong

and making a mistake caused me to behave in a way that is not natural to me.

2. I reacted from a belief system that goes something like "If I make these types of mistakes I am not good enough" and "She will think I do not respect her time if I do these things."

3. Because I made my decision from fear, I did not give her much to work with and she had to defend herself (her own fears coming into play).

4. Only when I took a step back and looked at all the moving parts, reflected and connected with my heart, did I pick up the phone to re-connect and own the decisions I had made.

5. Because there is trust in this relationship it was easy to resolve, yet if we were different people with a different relationship, this could have been really unhealthy.

Does any of this sound familiar?

> Through not choosing we become passengers in our own lives
>
> A. Bakkes

We often forget that everything we do is a choice. From the little smile to the big life decisions. The way we brush our teeth in the morning, the route we take to school, work, to the train or the bus. The hairstyle and clothes we wear. They are all decisions and we make them from different places and often we are not aware and conscious of the decisions we make. To make it even more interesting, we base a whole bunch of decisions on assumptions that become our truth (belief systems).

I have experienced that we sometimes do not choose because we actually do not think it matters or will make an impact. We could not be further from the truth. Every decision we make, no matter how seemingly small or insignificant, shapes our lives. The little decisions we make flow into more little decisions which flow into a way of living and behaving.

A few examples:

Trying to lose weight. The initial decision is often the "easy" one and the "big" decision. It is the little decisions every time after that, that will show results or not. It is saying yes to the healthy food, the daily intake of water and healthy life choices that shows achievement over a period of time. It is choosing the chocolate cake or the fizzy drink or the unhealthy choices that stops us from getting any results. It is the commitment of re-choosing that changes the way we behave.

Changing a bad habit. (e.g. quitting smoking or drinking less alcohol or stop biting your nails). The initial decision normally comes with some conviction. It is here that the place that we make our choices from makes a big difference. If I want to change my behaviour because I believe it will be good for me and that it is loving, it is far easier to stay committed and re-choose every day. It is when we make our decision from fear or judgement that it is hard to re-choose because we do not always believe in our choices.

Staying in an unhealthy relationship: There are times that we stay in abusive or unhealthy relationships because we "do not choose". People stay in unhappy marriages, friendships and jobs for years because the fear of the unknown and uncertainty is bigger than the pain and the discomfort they are experiencing. Not choosing is a choice. We are giving ourselves the message that we are not important enough for healthy love, relationships and work endeavours. It is the daily small choices to accept the unhealthy space that cause us to be anxious daily, become sick and have weak immune systems. When the situation is really intense we end up with depression, abuse and long-term illness.

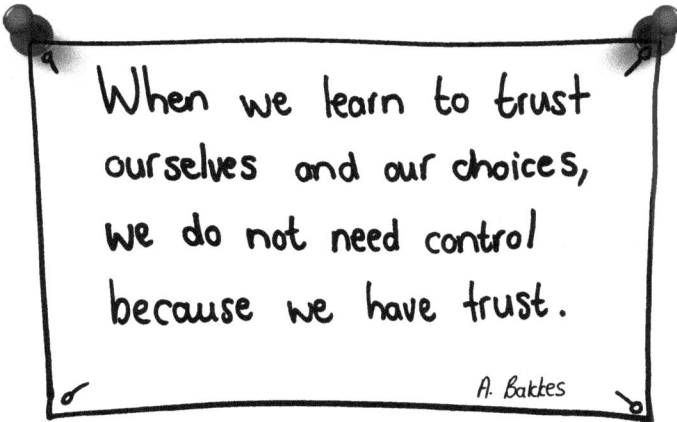

> When we learn to trust ourselves and our choices, we do not need control because we have trust.
>
> A. Bakkes

When we practise constant consistent conscious choice, we shape our life one decision at a time. The seemingly small decisions line up to carve out a life that is full of purpose and it puts you in the driver's seat of your life. If there is a need for control, the only person that is in control of our choice is us. We can control how we interpret information and what meaning we give to situations and events. Your choice is the one thing that no-one can do for you and no-one can take away from you. Remember that we need to recognise that our interpretation of the world is just that ... our interpretation. And our interpretation of the world is based on our fears, belief systems, memory and experiences. This is something we can change if we choose to.

When we choose to grow and not just change it means we can and will transcend our boundaries. When we choose growth and consistently choose it, this leads to behaving consistently with insight, making high-quality decisions and therefore living a high-quality life. This does not mean our lives will be without challenge. All it means is that we will choose how we deal with our challenges in the best and most insightful way we can in that moment.

So here is our ongoing growth challenge in life. Feel and feel deeply, and choose not to make our decisions from the fearful and anxious feelings. Become aware of them, accept that we have them and then choose from hope. Often it is not our decisions that change our lives and those around us, but the place we make those decisions from. Sit with the feelings of fear, anxiety, pain, loss, loneliness ... and choose not to make your choices from them. Feel them, let them go and choose from what gives you hope. Even in the most difficult and scary times there is hope, if we choose to see it.

We choose every day. I leave you with some guidelines on when we are able to grow and make our best decisions.

Table 5.4: Guidelines to help us choose

There is an element of certainty that we can identify	• Remember that we may not like the certainty we see. We might want it to be different from what it is. Remember that it is what it is, and if we can see that we can choose. • If you cannot find any certainty, find what gives you hope. Choosing from hope has endless possibilities. Hope is what graduates us from surviving into purposeful living.
We are aware of our feelings	• The moment we acknowledge our feelings we can choose what to do with them. • When we know where our feelings come from we can choose with internal wisdom and not from our fear memory and wounds. We can choose to heal.
When we are aware of our fears	• When we give our anxieties a label our brains can connect with our hearts and we make our best and most sustainable decisions.
When we invite curiosity and gratitude	• We cannot be anxious and afraid when we are truly curious. This is the childlike curiosity that looks out for possibility. • When we are grateful our immune system strengthens, our general wellbeing increases and our decisions are of a higher quality. • Gratitude and curiosity enable possibility out of uncertainty.

When our head and heart are aware of each other and in synch	• When we practise acknowledging our feelings, it is easier for the limbic brain and the neocortex to communicate and combine the emotions with logic and language. These decisions are our best.
When we can distinguish between fear memory and our current reality ... is this still true?	• When we are aware of our belief systems, fears and old ways of thinking, we can distinguish between our old memories and what is real in the moment. • By choosing from a perspective of accepting what is, the future can be changed and influenced. (Try and suspend the judgement.)
When we feel safe and/or secure	• Discover what, who and where you feel safe and create as much as you can of that in your life. • Make important decisions (that could look very small) from a space of hope and try to do it as often and consistently as possible. • Make a conscious effort to remember when and where and what circumstances make you feel safe, at ease and confident. Build a positive memory bank of when you feel safe.
We invite courage to see what is really there and not our judgement	• Initially it takes courage to choose and then some more courage to choose from love, gratitude and awareness. • The more we practise this, the more easily the unconscious competence increases and after consistent practice it becomes habit and a way of living. Anything is possible.
We give ourselves permission to choose	• We often forget that we are not only allowed to choose, but by not choosing we become passengers in our own lives. • With the permission to choose also comes the responsibility of commitment to self. When we choose from the heart and the head, the commitment comes naturally because we believe and trust in our choices.

> What support or anything else do you need to...
>
> Embrace your Anxiety?

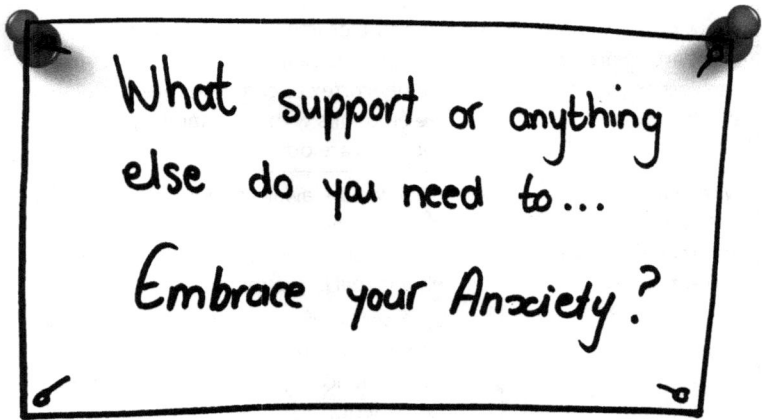

In Wrapping Up

"The best way to predict the future is to create it"[83]

I want to end where I started. If we just become aware of our anxiety, the causes and the way we interact with our feelings, we can choose from a place of hope rather than a place of fear and desperation.

In the last few weeks leading up to the completion of this book, I found myself so many times questioning myself: Do I practise what I preach? And the answer? Most of the time. There are times when my anxiety owns me and all I remember in that moment is: Feel it, feel it to the point of pain and do not choose from it. Sometimes I actually delay a decision because I have learnt by now that I do not make great decisions form anxiety. And of course there is part of me that judges the potential procrastination. All said and done, I hope that you took something from these pages that will enable you to live a richer fuller life with anxiety as a healthy friend and not a feared enemy.

May you listen to life's whispers and choose from hope in every small choice so that the big ones can take care of themselves. Blessings and love to you.

References

Anderson, D. & Anderson, M. 2005. *Coaching that counts: Harnessing the power of leadership coaching to deliver strategic value*. USA: Elsevier Butterworth – Heinemann.

Amin, A. *The 31 Benefits of Gratitude you didn't know about: How Gratitude can change your life*. [Accessed September 2016.]

Ashkanasy, N.M. & Daus, C. 2002. *Emotion in the workplace: The new challenge for managers*. *The academy of Management Executive*, **16**(1): 76 - 86.

Ashkanasy, N.M. & Nicholson, G.J. 2003. Climate of Fear in Organisational Settings: Construct Definition, Measurement and a Test of Theory. *Australian Journal of Psychology*, 55(1).

Association for Coaching. 2013. *Value of coaching*. [Online] Available: http://www. associationforcoaching.com [Accessed: 15 October 2012].

Brown, CB. 2012. *Daring greatly: How the courage to be vulnerable transforms the way we live, love, parent, and lead*. New York, NY: Gotham Books. p22.

Brown, P. & Hales, B. 2011. Developing leaders: Executive Education in Practice. *Neoroscience. New Science for New Leadership*, **5**: 36-41.

Brown, P., Swart, T. & Meyler, J. 2009. Emotional intelligence and the amygdala: towards the development of the concept of the limbic leader in executive coaching. *Neuro Leadership Journal*, **2**: 1-11.

Burgo, J. 2011. *The fear of change*. [Online] Available: http://www.afterpsychotherapy.com/the-fear-of-change/ [Accessed: 13 November 2012].

Canadian Institute of Neurosciences, Mental Health and Addiction. 2012. *The Brain from Top to Bottom*. [Online] Available: http://thebrain.mcgill.ca/flash/d/d_05/d_05_cr/d_05_cr_her/d_05_cr_her.html [Accessed: 12 November 2012].

Caine, R.N, & Caine, G. 1990. *Making Connections: Teaching and the Human Brain*. Nashville, TN: Incentive Publications.

Charles D. Kerns, PhD, MBA. 2006 Gratitude at Work: Counting your blessings will benefit yourself and your organization. *Graziadio Business Review*. Volume 9, Issue 4. [Online] Available: https://gbr.pepperdine.edu/2010/08/gratitude-at-work/ [Accessed 17 January 2017].

Charles, D Kerns, PhD, MBA, Graziadio School of Business and Management 2014.

Changing Minds. 2012. *Judgement Sampling*. [Online] Available: http://changingminds. org/explanations/research/sampling/judgment_sampling.html [Accessed: 24 November 2012].

Chapman, L. & Stout Rostron, S. 2010. *Integrated Experiential Coaching: Becoming an executive coach*. London: Karnak Books.

Collard, C. & Walsh, J. 2008. *Sensory Awareness Mindfulness Training in Coaching: Accepting Life's Challenges*. [Online] Available http://link.springer.com/article/ Accessed: 12 October 2012.

Cope, M. 2004. *The Seven C's of Coaching: The definitive guide to collaborative coaching*. Great Britain: Pearson Education Limited.

Deming, W.E. 1982. *Quality, Productivity, and Competitive Position*. Cambridge, MA. Massachusetts Institute of Technology, Centre for Advanced Engineering Study.

Dictionary.com. [Online] Available: http://www.dictionary.com/browse/relief [Accessed 17 January 2017].

Do2Learn, 2013. Emotions Color Wheel. [Online] Available: http://do2learn.com/organizationtools/EmotionsColorWheel/index.htm [Accessed 17 January 2017].

Doidge, N. 2007. *The brain that changes itself: Stories of personal triumph from the frontiers of brain science*. England: Penguin Books Ltd.

Downs, A. 2002. *Secrets of an executive coach: Proven methods for helping leaders excel under pressure*. New York: American Management Association.

Drucker, P. BrainyQuote.com, Xplore Inc, 2017. [Online] Available: https://www.brainyquote.com/quotes/authors/p/peter_drucker.html [Accessed 17 January 2017].

Dunbar, A. 2010. *Essential Life Coaching Skills*. USA: Routledge.

Emmons, R.A. & McCullough, M.E. 2004. *The Psychology of Gratitude, An introduction*. Oxford University Press.

Explorable.com. 2012. *Convenience Sampling*. [Online] Available: http://explorable.com/convenience-sampling.html [Accessed: 24 November 2012].

Ferlic, K. 2006. *Fear of the unknown: A Realising your Unlimited Creativity discussion topic*. [Online] Available: http://ryuc.info/common/creation_process/fear_unknown.htm [Accessed: 1 November 2012].

Franken, E.F. 1994. *Human Motivation*. California: Brooks/Cole Publishing Company.

Flaherty, J. 2005. *Coaching: evoking excellence in others*. USA: Elsevier Butterworth-Heinemann.

Folk, J. & Folk, M. BScN. April 2015. 'Anxiety Attacks (panic attacks) and Anxiety Disorder: Information, help, support, and counseling/therapy'. Anxietycentre.com. [Online] Available: http://www.anxietycentre.com. [Accessed October 2016].

Gilbert, D. 2006. *Stumbling on Happiness*. Alfred, A. Knopf, USA

Griffiths, B. 2009. The paradox of change: How to coach while dealing with fear and uncertainty. *Industrial and Commercial Training*, **41**(2): 97–101.

Goleman, D., 1996. Emotional Intelligence. Why It Can Matter More than IQ. *Learning*, **24**(6), pp 49-50. Passionate Spirituality Review Notes prepared by Ron Bonar – January 2000 Engulfed.

Goleman, D. 1998. What makes a leader? *Harvard Business Review*. November-December 1998. [Online] Available: http://richardreoch.info/wp-content/uploads/2016/05/What-Makes-a-Leader.pdf [Accessed 17 January 2017].

Kelvens, C. 1997. *Fear and Anxiety*. Northridge: California State University. [Online] Available: http://www.csun.edu/~vcpsy00h/students/fear.htm [Accessed: 3 October 2012].

Kerns, C.D. PhD, MBA. Counting your blessings will benefit yourself and your organisation: Gratitude at work: Volume 9 Issue 4, 2006

Kinder, A., Hughes, R. & Cooper, C.L. 2008. *Employee Well-being Support: A Workplace Resource*. England: John Wiley & Sons Ltd.

Kline, N. 1999. *Time to Think: Listening to ignite the human mind*. London: Cassell Illustrated.

Knight, S. 1995. *NLP at Work: Neuro Linguistic Programming: The difference that makes a difference in business*. London: Nicholas Brealey Publishing.

Learn2Develop. 2009. *Thoughts from the world of learning and development*. [Online] Available: http://learn2develop.blogspot.com/2009/10/kolb-is-it-useful.html [Accessed: 21 October 2012].

Le Doux, J. 1998. The Neural Circuits Underlying Anxiety and Fear. *Fear and the Brain: Where Have We Been, and Where Are We Going?* New York: Society of Biological Psychiatry.

McGee, P.E. 2012. 'The 7 Humor Habits Program. Finally! A Humor Training Program that Works!'. *The Laughter Remedy*. [Online] Available: http://www.laughterremedy.com/ [Accessed 17 January 2017].

Merriam-Webster Incorporated. 2013. *Definition of fear*. [Online] Available: http://www. merriam-webster.com/dictionary/fear [Accessed: 21 October 2012].

Mills-Scofield, D. 2012. Hope is a Strategy (Well, sort of), *Harvard Business Review*, 09 October, 2012.

Morin, A. 2014. '7 Scientifically Proven Benefits Of Gratitude That Will Motivate You To Give Thanks Year Round'. *Forbes*. [Online] Available: http://www.forbes.com/ sites/amymorin/2014/11/23/7-scientifically-proven-benefits-of-gratitude-that-will-motivate-you-to-give-thanks-year-round/#2196ebbf6800 [Accessed 23 August 2016].

Native Remedies LLC. 2012. *The Natural Choice*. [Online] Available: http://www. nativeremedies.com/ailment/overcoming-fears-info.html [Accessed: 13 December 2012].

Neenan, M. & Palmer, S. 2012. *Cognitive Behavioural Coaching in Practice: An Evidence Based Approach*. Canada: Routledge.

Nel, C. 2012: *The Practice and Virtues of High Impact Leadership and Teaming*. [Online] Available: http://www.villageofleaders.co.za/wp-content/uploads/2013/06/The-Practice-and-Virtues-of-Leadership-Article-by-Christo-Nel-2012.pdf [Accessed 17 January 2017]..

Oxford University Press. 2012. *Oxford Dictionaries: The world's most trusted dictionaries*. [Online] Available: http://oxforddictionaries.com/definition/english/anxiety [Accessed: 17 October 2012].

PageInsider.com. 2013. *The Triune Brian*. [Online] Available: http://pbmo.wordpress. com/2011/05/21/triune-brain/) [Accessed: 18 November 2012].

Personal-Coaching-Information.com. 2012. *Grow Coaching Model*. [Online] Available: http://www.personal-coaching-information.com/grow-coaching-model.html [Accessed: 22 November 2012].

Rock, D. 2009. *Our brain at work: Strategies for overcoming distraction, regaining focus, and working smarter all day long*. NY: HarperCollins.

Rogers, C.R. 1961. *On Becoming a Person: A Therapist's view of Psychotherapy*. London: Constable & Company Ltd.

Roy, S. 2010. *The Psychology of Fear*. [Online] Available: http://www.futurehealth.org/ populum/page.php?f=The-Psychology-of-Fear-by-Saberi-Roy-100903-820.html [Accessed: 15 October 2013].

Selfgrowth.com. 2013. *The Online Self Improvement Community*. [Online] Available: http://www. selfgrowth.com/articles/Definition_Personal_Values.html [Accessed: 2 October 2012].

Seligman, M.E.P. 1975. *Helplessness on development, depression & death*. New York: W.H. Freeman and Company.

Skiffington, S. & Zeus, P. 2003. *Behavioural Coaching: How to build sustainable personal and organisational strength*. Australia: The McGraw-Hill Companies.

Smith, M., Segal, R., & Segal, J. 2012. *Stress: Symptoms, Causes and Relief*. [Online] Available: http://www.helpguide.org/mental/stress_signs.html [Accessed: 3 November 2012].

Snoden, D.J. & Boone, M.E. 2007. A learner's framework for decision making. *Harvard Business Review*, 2007 Issue.

Stanford Encyclopedia of Philosophy. 2010. *Existentialism*. [Online] Available: http://plato. stanford.edu/entries/existentialism [Accessed: 17 November 2012].

Stout Rostron, S. 2009. *Business Coaching: Wisdom and Practice*. Randburg: Knowres Publishing.

Thongsukmag, J. 2003. *Fear in the Workplace: The Relationships among Sex, Self-efficacy, and Coping Strategies*. Virginia: Virginia State University.

Tucker-Ladd, C. 2011. *Psychological Self-Help*. [Online] Available: http:// psychologicalselfhelp.org/Bibliography/ [Accessed: 7 October 2012].

Valerio, A.M. & Lee, R.J. 2005. *Executive Coaching: A guide for the HR professional*. San Francisco: Pfeiffer.

Wai-Packard, B. 2012. *Definition of Mentoring*. Mount Holyoke College. [Online] Available: http://ehrweb.aaas.org/sciMentoring/Mentor_Definitions_Packard.pdf [Accessed: 21 November 2012].

WebMD, LLC. 2012. *The effects of stress on your body*. [Online] Available: http://www.webmd. com/mental-health/effects-of-stress-on-your-body [Accessed: 15 November 2012].

Whitmore, J. 2009. *Coaching for Performance: Growing human potential and purpose*. London: Nicholas Brealey Publishing.

Whitworth, W., Kimsey-House, K., Kimsey-House, P. & Sandal. P. 2007. *Co-Active Coaching: new skills for coaching people towards success in work and life*. California: Davies-Black Publishing.

Williams, M & Penmann, D. 2011. *Mindfulness, a practical guide to finding peace in a frantic world*. Great Britain: Piatkus

Winters, J. 2012. *Why we fear the unknown*. [Online] Available: http://www.psychologytoday. com/articles/200305/why-we-fear-the-unknown [Accessed: 29 November 2012].

Womenshealth.gov. 2010. *Stress and your health fact sheet*. [Online] Available: http:// womenshealth.gov/publications/our-publications/fact-sheet/stress-your-health. cfm [Accessed: 21 November 2010].

Woolwine, H. 2004. *Extreme stress, fear linked to mental illness*. [Online] Available: http:// www.musc.edu/catalyst/archive/2004/co7-9extreme.html [Accessed: 10 December 2012].

Endnotes

1   Carl Rogers, 1961.
2   Folk & Folk, 2015:2.
3   Tucker–Ladd, 2011:3.
4   C.R. Renolts & R.W. Kamphaus, 2013.
5   Kinder et al., 2008:240.
6   Kinder et al., 2008:240.
7   Neenan and Palmer, 2012:154.
8   Tucker–Ladd, 2011:13.
9   Kelvens, 1997.
10 Kelvens, 1997.
11 Oxford University Press, 2012.
12 Kelvens, 1997.
13 Merriam-Webster Incorporated, 2013.
14 Native Remedies, 2012.
15 *The Merriam-Webster Learner's Dictionary*
16 Snowden, 2007
17 Snowden, 2007
18 Rock, 2009:121.
19 Gilbert, 2006
20 Brown, 2012:22.
21 Rogers, 1961:47.
22 Rogers, 1961:51.
23 Brown, 2012:33.
24 Rogers, 1961:50.
25 Deborah Mills-Scofield, *Harvard Business Review*, 2012.
26 Brown, 2012:126.
27 Rogers, 1961:56.
28 Brown, 2012:12.
29 Brown, 2012: 8.
30 Rubinstein, 2016 (when I accessed it)
31 Wikipedia, 2016.
32 Bakkes, 2013
33 Kierkegaard (Nel 2012)
34 Brown, 2012:161.
35 Rock, 2009:129.
36 Rock, 2009:81.
37 Rogers, 1961.
38 O'Brien, 2016.
39 Williams & Penmann, 2011.
40 Williams & Penmann, 2011:19.
41 Rock, 2009:81.
42 Brown, 2012:145.
43 Kline, 1999.
44 Kline, 1999.
45 Nel, 2012.
46 Koestenbaum & Kierkegaard, 2012. (Nell 2012).
47 Seneca, 2004.
48 Maraboli, 2016 (when I accessed it).
49 Forbes, 2014.
50 Emmons, 2004.
51 McGee, 2012.
52 Happierhuman.com, 2015.
53 Dictionary.com.
54 Kerns, 2006.
55 Kinder et al., 2008:240.
56 Neenan & Palmer, 2012:154.
57 Kelvens, 1997.
58 Oxford University Press, 2012.
59 Kelvens, 1997.
60 Merriam-Webster Incorporated, 2013.
61 Native Remedies, 2012.
62 Tucker–Ladd, 2011.
63 Tucker–Ladd, 2011:3.
64 Kelvens, 1997.
65 Knight, 1995:85-87.
66 Kinder et al., 2008:240.
67 Selfgrowth.com, 2013.
68 Kline, 1999:18.
69 Ashkanasy & Daus, 2002:78.
70 Knight, 1995:85-87.
71 Rock, 2009:79.
72 MacLean, 1960.
73 PageInsider, 2013.
74 Brown & Hales, 2011:39.
75 Brown & Hales, 2011:39.
76 Doidge, 2007.
77 Do2Learn, 2013.
78 Goleman, 1998.
79 Goleman, 1996.
80. Brown & Hales, 2011:40-41.
81 Deming, 1982:33.
82 Rock, 2009.
83 Drucker, 2010.

Index

A

acceptance, 27–28, 32–35, 38, 43, 46, 48, 52, 58, 60, 62, 96
  unconditional, 32
acceptance in human psychology, 32
acceptance perspective, 30
acceptance steps, 27
acohol intake, 103, 106, 122
addiction, 98
adrenaline, 54, 105
adults, 81
  young, 14
adventure, 83, 87
Agile coach, 10, 23
Agile Coaching Institute, 30
Agile facilitation, 60
agitation, 104
agreement, 32, 34, 38, 96
  equal, 52
anger, 44, 100
anxiety, 4–5, 8–21, 23, 25–27, 29–31, 33, 37–41, 51–54, 56, 59–60, 64–65, 67, 86–91, 95–106, 126
  chronic, 14
  constant, 106
  decisions from, 126
  experience, 11–12, 67, 88
  identifying, 86
  minimising, 64
  prolonged, 8
  underlying, 15
anxiety and fear, 40, 86–87, 105, 107, 111, 119
anxiety-filled life, 2
anxiety levels, 17, 33, 102
anxiety provoking, 20
anxiety-related feelings, 105
anxious dependence, 68
anxious feelings, 124
arbitration, 67
ARIA (Awareness, Reflection, Insight, Action), 120

assumptions, 11, 23, 41, 74, 82–83, 91–93, 109, 122
  limiting, 92
attachment, 45–48, 52, 101–102, 109
  level of, 45, 52
  limiting, 48
autopilot mode, 53, 55, 64, 102

B

balance, 80, 84, 97, 102, 104, 106
behaviour, 11–13, 27, 39, 41, 46, 48, 51, 53, 56, 59–62, 69–70, 89–92, 104, 106–116, 118
  actual, 41
  autopilot, 53
  child's, 112
  citizenship, 71
  human, 110
  observed, 58
  outward, 115–117
  person/s, 114
  team's, 53
behavioural changes, long-lasting, 118
behavioural choices, best, 110
behavioural evidence, 117
behavioural patterns, 51, 94
behavioural symptoms, 105–106
behaviour change, 52
beliefs, 25, 91–92
belief systems, 7, 13, 39, 41, 50–51, 64–65, 88–89, 91–96, 98, 101–102, 109, 111, 114, 116, 118, 121–123, 125
  guide, 91
  inform, 92, 95, 96
  limiting, 39
  mould, 92
body language, 111
boundaries, 10, 18, 123
  clear, 18
brain, 7, 15, 20–21, 40–41, 44, 51, 77, 86, 89–90, 94, 97–100, 102, 108–109, 119, 124

brain patterns, new, 76
brain plasticity, 111
brain stem, 97
BS, *see* belief system
building block, 101
bullet-proof, 96, 112
burnout, 14
  long-term, 116

C

cancer, 3–5, 7, 10, 19, 22–23, 25, 76, 78, 94
  chemotherapy, 3–4
  colon, 80
  contract, 5, 6, 19
  fighting, 72, 80
cancer cells, 7
cancer diagnoses, 3, 72, 77
cancer patients, 72, 80
cancer survival, 80, 94
capabilities, 13, 87
capacity, 55, 64, 68
  brain's, 102
  human, 108
  predictive, 21
career, 66, 69, 71, 73
change, 19–21, 26–28, 31–34, 40–41, 43, 46, 56, 64–67, 69–70, 76–77, 93–95, 98–99, 101–102, 116–118, 122–124
change ignites, 46
chaos, 17, 19, 20
check-ups, 10
  regular, 72–73
child's confidence, 85
choices, 10, 12, 15–16, 18, 22, 24, 26–27, 39, 41–42, 52–54, 56, 64, 91, 119, 121–125
  active, 16
  best, 119
  disastrous, 100
  liberating, 26
  quality, 61
  small, 126
  unhealthy, 122
Circadian rhythms, 108

clients, 46, 53, 55, 89, 106, 110, 120
clothes, 33, 115, 121
coaching conversations, 5
coaching diploma, 19
coaching practice, 20, 28, 86
coaching sessions, 1, 29
cognitive brain, 98
cognitive symptoms, 104
comfort zone, 83
commitment, 1, 12, 122, 125
  lifelong, 7
companies, 46, 66, 92, 119
compassion, 24, 29, 39–40, 57, 62, 83, 85
competencies, 33
complexity, 3, 14, 16–18, 20–21, 54, 64, 67, 89, 116
  intense, 3
  medical, 6
complex sequence, 14, 87
complex world, 18, 98, 100
complicated contexts, 18
components, 21, 26
  informal, 21
  subjective, 21
concentration, 84
conflict, 44, 114
conflict resolution, 67
connections, 15, 60, 67, 69, 110
  easy, 61
  human, 59–60, 68
  real, 29
conscious choice, 53, 78
  consistent, 123
conscious competence, 84
conscious incompetence, 83
consciousness, 42, 98
context, 4, 8, 37, 117
  chaotic, 19
  complex, 19
  individual, 18
  personal, 104
continuous practice of mindful observation, 58
continuous setbacks, 4
continuous uncertainty, 4

control, 2, 13, 19, 23, 32, 56, 64, 78, 89, 96, 102, 112, 123
  cognitive, 56
  complete, 112
  perceived, 5, 64
conversation, 3, 5, 32, 54, 62–63, 67, 80, 85, 101, 103–104, 114–115, 120
  daily, 78
  difficult, 67
  good, 117
  internal, 41, 111, 117
  pivotal, 66
corporates, 6, 27
corrective action, 18
counselling, 13
courage, 1, 24, 33, 38, 48, 60, 62, 90, 95, 125
courageous, 24, 38, 67
courageous decisions, 3
creativity, 68, 107
cues, 106
  physical, 111
culture, 64, 68, 91–92
culture work, 27
curiosity, 31, 57–60, 82, 124
  childlike, 124
curve, 81
  upward, 8
Cynefin Framework, 17

D

danger, 88, 97–98, 100, 111
  awareness of, 15, 88
  minimise, 64, 111
  perceived, 88
  potential, 15, 20, 88
  warning of, 12, 88
decisions, 1–5, 18–21, 23–24, 26, 41, 44, 46–48, 50–52, 58, 68, 70–71, 90–93, 98, 100, 121–126
  best, 23, 51, 56, 124
  complex, 108
  everyday, 26
  high-quality, 123
  holistic, 119

limiting, 50
little, 122
low-quality, 20
partner's, 112
small, 26, 100
social, 94
sustainable, 124
defeatedness, 32
defensiveness, 113
delivery, 47
  actual, 46
depression, 70, 104–105, 123
desperation, 5, 70–71, 126
despondence, 23, 55
destination, 78–79, 86–87
  new unknown, 87
diet, 115
  going on a, 115
  healthy, 103
different truths, 67–68
discipline, 12, 75, 85
discomfort, 15–16, 21, 24, 40, 60, 74, 86, 109, 111, 122
  life's, 1
  physical, 8
discoveries, 6, 48, 57, 83
disorders, 12, 61
  generalised anxiety, 13
distress, 13–14, 74, 87–88
diversity contexts, 67
dizziness, 105
domains, 17–18
dress code, 114
  appropriate, 114
drive, 2, 38, 66, 78, 87, 90–91, 104
  sex, 106
drugs, 106

E

eating habits, 33
effectiveness, 46
effort, 84–85
  conscious, 125
effortlessness, 11, 85, 114
electrical activity, 51

electromagnetic field generator, 108
elements
    key, 37, 40, 54
    limiting, 32, 49
    traumatic, 70
embarrassment, 115
embarrasssment, public, 89
Embracing Anxiety, 2, 4, 6, 8, 10, 12, 14,
        16, 18, 24, 28–30, 40, 42, 68, 80–
        126
Embracing Anxiety Model, 1, 4–5, 81, 89,
        97
Embracing Anxiety Model and processes,
        37
Embracing Anxiety workshops, 44, 63
emotional balance, 108
    brain, 101
    labour, 92
    outcome, 11
    reactions, 12, 87
    responses, 13, 87
    roller coaster, 6
    self-awareness, 101
emotional state, 119
    unpleasant, 14, 87
emotional symptoms, 104
emotions, 3, 5, 15, 18, 41, 54–56, 77, 81,
        86, 88–89, 92, 97–102, 106–107,
        109–111, 117–118
    constant, 87
    negative, 26, 74, 110
    painful, 56
    primary, 100
    sharing, 105
    strong, 15, 88, 100
    toxic, 70
emotions colour wheel, 99
employee turnover, reducing, 71
energy, 6, 20–21, 32, 60, 65, 69, 73, 80, 89,
        100, 104, 106
    nervous, 106
    physical, 71
energy inwards, 100
environments, 14, 17, 19, 28, 60, 75, 87–
        88, 110
    corporate, 6

    emotional, 4
    measured, 5
    spatial, 104
everyday life, 17, 20, 92
excitement, 82, 85, 87
exercise regime, 33
exercises, 12, 15, 18, 29–31, 34, 48, 58, 60,
        75, 90, 94–95, 99
    regular, 73
    standard, 30
experience, 18–19, 33–34, 60–61, 68, 70,
        72, 80, 82–83, 85–88, 90, 92, 107,
        110, 115, 117
expressive suppression, 116

F

facilitator, 10
factors, 14, 16, 24, 44–45, 71, 78, 109
    common, 72
    internal, 83
    motivational, 14
    psychological, 72
failure, 26, 44, 46, 61, 94, 96, 112
fear and anxiety, 4, 13, 89, 91, 98–99, 111
feared enemy, 126
fear memory, 111, 124–125
fear of failure, 96, 112
feedback, 39, 47, 60, 63, 84, 117–118
frequent colds, 106
fight fear, 80
fight/flight, 108
filters, 50–51
fit, 11, 16, 33, 50, 115
Five Steps, 83, 85, 87, 89, 91, 93, 95, 97,
        99, 101, 103, 105, 107, 109, 111
flawed baseline assumptions, 120
focus, 14, 18, 27, 56, 58, 64, 73, 75–76, 78,
        85–86, 91, 94, 104, 112, 120
food, 115
    best, 115
    healthy, 122
freeze responses, 97
friendship conduct, 113
friendships, 70, 92, 122
    guiding, 27

functional psychopathology, 61

G

Generalised Anxiety Disorder (GAD), 13
gifts, 6, 9–10, 23, 60, 117
giving/receiving, 108, 114
goal, 14, 18–19, 38, 89, 94
  new, 9
goal achievement, 71, 73
goal-setting, 89
golden phrases, 117
golden thread, 54
grateful behaviour, 71
gratitude, 6, 9–10, 26, 38, 40–41, 68–75, 77–80, 83, 99, 101, 124–125
gratitude exercise, 72
  daily, 76
gratitude journals, 71
group coaching sessions, 44
growth, 9, 15, 25, 27–28, 39, 41, 50, 73, 76, 81, 84, 92, 123–124
growth mindset, 71
guilt, 7, 44, 120

H

habits, 125
  bad, 122
  good, 100
  positive, 39
happiness, 68–70, 76, 100
healing, 6, 77, 105
health, 69, 72–73, 76, 78, 94, 112
  children's, 7–8
  good, 78
heart, 24, 69, 81, 100, 121, 124–125
heart attack, 89
heartbeat, 97
  rapid, 105
hectic schedules, 120
higher-order thinking, 97
higher quality decisions, 30
high tension, 17
high turbulence, 17
holistic model, 97

honesty, 66, 68, 90
  gentle, 38
hormones, feel-good, 76
human beings, 1–2, 18, 20, 29, 33, 61, 63, 91, 98, 100
human brain, 98
human growth, 58
human mind, 61
human psychology, 32
human reaction, 106
humour, 72–73

I

immune system, 8, 22, 72–73, 77, 106, 124
  low, 7
  low-functioning, 8
  weak, 123
implementation, 47
impulses, 54–55
incentive schemes, 66
incompetence, 47, 82
increased health, 73
increased insight, 58
increased possible choices, 58
increased sleep, 73
indebtedness, 74
independence, 80
individuals, 7, 71
inexperience, 18
infections, 4, 6
information, 15, 19–20, 44, 48, 80, 97–98, 102, 108, 113–114, 117–119, 123
information integration process, 15
infrastructure department, 66
insecurities, 46
insight, 20, 34, 39–40, 46, 49, 51, 53–56, 118, 120, 123
  gain, 34, 48, 51, 119
  limited, 53
instinctual response, 15, 88
integration, 15
  adaptive, 109
intelligence, 76, 103, 108
  emotional, 101

intact, 100
interaction, 14, 21, 67, 114
  interpersonal, positive, 71
interpretation, 56, 58, 75, 102, 123
introspection, 23
intuition, 106, 108
invisible domain, 17
irritability, 104
irritable bowel syndrome, 103

J

journal, 21, 34–35, 48, 58, 75–76, 90, 95
journey, 1–5, 7, 9, 12, 28–29, 47, 59–60,
      73, 77
  human, 43
  life's, 12, 46, 50
joy, 6, 22, 25–26, 70
  numb, 98
judge, 7, 11, 14, 28, 31, 33–34, 38, 44, 48–
      49, 51–53, 56, 92, 118, 126
judgement, 2, 24, 27–28, 30, 38, 40,
      43–47, 49–52, 56, 59–61, 65, 83,
      92–93, 101–102, 125
  level of, 27, 45, 50
  little, 56, 95
  no, 43
  spatial, 104
  suspend, 39, 58, 64, 95
  suspended, 27, 31, 38, 40–41, 43
judgement exacerbates disconnection,
      49
judgement, limiting, 43

K

knee-jerk reactions, 119
knowledge, 21, 76, 84

L

lack of control, 67
language, 15–16, 21, 29, 39, 60, 87, 125
  basic, 15
  human, 98
  self-judging, 31

language perspective, 43
leaders, 33, 35, 50, 61, 66
  better, 71
  senior, 46
leadership decisions, 18
leadership styles, 50, 111
learning, 60, 81–84
  how difficult or how easy, 82
  phases of, 81, 86
  stages of, 81
learning process, 6, 22–23, 25, 27, 41, 81,
      83, 85, 109, 126
lessons, 6, 9
  life-lasting, 69
life choices, healthy, 122
life contribution, 66
life's challenges, 25
limbic brain, 97–98, 125
listening, 62–63, 68
  active, 65
live happier, 80
logistics, 8, 55
loneliness, 104, 124
long-term illness, 123
long-term increased health, 75
love, 6–7, 9, 24, 26, 38, 40–41, 55, 57, 59,
      61–62, 65, 67, 76–78, 107–108,
      125–126
  healthy, 122
  practical, 38, 59, 61, 63–65
  romantic, 59
love in motion, 59, 63, 67
  elements of, 64–65
love made practical, 59
loving, 2, 6, 27, 33, 67, 110, 116, 122
loving space, 2, 115–116

M

magic, 57, 64
  real, 40
mammalian brain, 98
management, 73
  crisis, 17
  micro, 46
management coaching, 5

managers, 53, 71
manifestation, 27
  outward, 2, 24, 41
  practical, 61
mantras, 77–78
marriage, 7, 117–118
marriages, unhappy, 122
materialistic, 73
medical fraternity, 3
medical health industry, 5
medical solution, 7
medical world, 2
memory, 70, 100, 123, 125
memory bank, positive, 125
mental disorders, 13
mental health, 98
metabolism, 108
mindful emotions, 100
mindfulness, 54, 101
mindful observation, 31, 52–56, 58, 90, 95, 120
mind fuses, 54
misconception, 33
misinterpreting information, 110
misjudge, 104
mode, 55–56
  being, 53
  doing, 52
model, 4–5, 15, 17, 21, 37, 39–43, 45, 47, 49, 51, 53, 59, 61–63, 69–71, 86
model context, 15
model gratitude, 71
model suspended judgement, 40
moodiness, 104
motion, 52, 59, 64–65, 67

N

nationalities, 60
negative feelings, 57
neighbourhood, 83
neocortex, 97–98, 100, 125
nervousness, 14, 87, 106
networks, 70–71
neural pathways, 76

new, 99
Neuroleadership Institute, 20
neuroplasticity, 41, 94, 99
Neurosciences, 15, 98
non-violent communication, 117
nutritionist, 103

O

observation, 31, 38, 40–41, 50, 52, 54, 56, 58, 90, 101
observation work, 116
openness, 62, 66, 68
optimism, 26, 69, 72–73
ordered domain, 17
organisational profitability, increasing, 71
organisations, 17, 71, 92
outcome, 9, 14, 30, 34, 45, 48–49, 58, 60, 67, 75, 87, 90, 95, 113, 115
  clear, 19
  key, 71
  perceivable, 17
out-of-control, 23
outward action, 76
over- judge, 53
overwhelmedness, 105

P

pains, 72, 74, 103, 105, 122, 124, 126
  chest, 103, 105
  continuous neck, 103
  numb, 98
panic attacks, 11
parenting, 18, 27, 47, 110, 113
parents, 33, 35, 49, 61, 78, 110
partnership, 9
passive resentfulness, 5
past experience, 50
path, 2
  linear, 26
patience, 12, 84–85
patients, 72, 80
perceptions, 12–13, 46, 58, 88–89, 91, 111
permission, 33, 39, 41, 125
personal affirmations, 78

personal benefits, 71
personal experience, 21–22, 25, 40
personality, 7, 73, 83, 93, 111
personality & social, 69
personal power, 108
perspective, 34, 67–68, 125
    changed, 73
    cognitive, 89, 91
    healthy, 71
    new, 52, 93
philosophy, 5
physical ability, 7
physical damage, 115
physical expressions, 103
physical symptoms, 13
physiological regulation, 108
pillars, 43, 45, 47, 49, 51, 53, 55, 57, 59, 61,
        63, 65, 67, 69, 71
post traumatic growth, 70, 73
Post Traumatic Stress Disorder, 70
potential behaviour, 112–114
potential danger lights, 120
potential supportive limiting belief sys-
        tem, 96–97, 112–114
power, 2, 41, 98, 107
practice
    consistent, 84, 125
    daily, 12
    doing, 31
practising gratitude, 68–70, 73, 77, 79–80
practising gratitude changes, 75
practising love, 40, 68
practising optimism, 73
practising self-love, 62
pre-conceived conclusions, 57
pre-decided pattern, 55
pre-determined thinking, 56
predisposition, 13
pressure, 5, 13, 53, 87, 89
problems, 12, 15, 51, 54, 56, 63, 69, 71, 93
    memory, 104
    new, 93
    personal, 54
procrastinating, 106, 126
productivity, 66, 71
    higher, 73

professionals, 8, 14
prolonged stress, 14
psychologist, 9

Q

quality insight, 58
quitting smoking, 122

R

racing thoughts, 104
rationalise, 113
raw feelings, 54
reflective observation, 53
regret, 44, 70, 119
relationship assumption, 9
relationship goal, 9
relationship patterns, 9
relationship resilience, 9
relationships, 7–9, 13, 25, 27, 51, 64, 67,
        70, 73, 98, 106–108, 111–112, 116–
        117, 121–122
    abusive, 111
    clear, 18
    close, 70
    community, 71
    intimate, 110
    romantic, 70
    unhealthy, 122
reptilian brain, 97
research, 13–14, 21, 24–25, 40, 70–72, 77,
        89, 91–92, 110–111
research definitions, 16
research positions, 24
resentment, 44, 70, 110
resilience, 4, 6, 15, 16, 21–26, 68, 73
    practising, 22
    present, 21
resilience-in-training process, 23
resilience-strengthening time, 22
resilience training, ever-continuing, 23
resources, 13, 31, 34, 48, 58, 75, 87, 90, 95
responsibilities, 106, 125
    neglecting, 106

reward, 64, 111
reward policies, 66
risks, 7, 24
  emotional, 24
role, 27, 46, 60, 66, 72, 77–78, 80, 83, 87

S

sadness, 100
scary, 9, 11, 20, 23, 53, 67
schools, 6, 67, 121
second nature, 85
self, 7, 25, 28, 30, 35, 38, 40, 43, 45, 53, 57,
        104, 108, 115–116, 118
self-acceptance, 25, 29, 33
self-awareness, 5, 19, 26, 28–29, 32, 46,
        49–50, 56, 59, 66, 99
self-discovery, 28
self-esteem, 73, 106
self-healing tips, 108
self-insight, 54
self-judgement, 2, 29
self-love, 7, 61, 68, 77, 83
self-loving activity, 115
self-loving thoughts, 76
self-trust, 25, 73
sensations, bodily, 54–55
sense of humour, 72–73
sense of loneliness and isolation, 104
sexuality, 108
shame, 44, 113, 115
situation, 12–13, 30, 32–33, 45–46, 48–52,
        56–57, 79, 87–89, 96–97, 102, 104–
        106, 109–110, 114, 116–120, 123
  life-threatening, 105
skill, 16, 21, 65–66, 82–86
  actual, 85
  decision-making, 20
  key, 18
  mental, 81
  new, 81–85, 114
  reflective, 34, 48
small businesses, 67
small choices, daily, 123
social capital, 69
social situation, 104

soul decisions, 3
space, 10, 14, 18–19, 53, 61, 64, 74, 99,
        125
  complex, 18
  grateful, 2
  healthy, 1, 9
  integrated, 100
  living, 112
  mindful, 100
  simple, 18
  unhealthy, 101, 123
  unhealthy drive, 116
speaking, public, 88
spirituality, 108
spiritual lesson, 83
spoken intent, 67
  open, 67
stress, 12–14, 40, 70, 72, 86–88, 91, 103,
        105, 108–109, 111
  short-term, 14
  substituting post traumatic, 73
success, 26, 32, 84, 94, 96, 112
  professional, 10
suppression, 106, 116
survival, 3, 5, 7, 77, 97, 100, 108
  children's, 9
survival mode, 6
survival signal, 12, 88
surviving, 7, 124
symptoms, 13
  physical, 39, 105–106
systems
  alarm, 13, 89
  cardiovascular, 77
  functional, 98
  human, 53
  liberating belief, 39, 95
  limbic, 56, 98, 110
  limiting belief, 39, 92, 95, 120
  new belief, 95–96
  old belief, 93
  possible belief, 112
  supportive, 94
  supportive belief, 96
systems thinking, 18

T

team, 46, 61, 66, 110–111
  executive, 46–47
  sports, 61
team dynamics, 66
team's gratitude, 66
temporary mental event, 57
tension, 12, 61, 66–67, 88
  internal, 110
therapy, 13
  aversion, 20
thinking, 30, 33, 38, 40, 51–56, 58, 61–62,
    67–68, 78, 85, 91, 93, 98, 100–101,
    104
thinking brain, 98
thinking partner, 95
thinking partnership, 63
thinking patterns, 58, 104
thinking process, 98
threat, 101, 111
tools, 12–13, 26, 39, 41, 59
  long-term, 40
  practical, 13
training alliance, 60
training session, 51
trauma, 50, 72, 92–93
  intense personal, 1
traumatic events, 21
tribal association, 108
trust, 9, 15, 19, 23–26, 64, 73, 77–78, 95,
    105–106, 121, 125
  active, 25
truth, 52, 57, 67–68, 92, 94, 109–111, 122
  common, 67
  internal, 114
  unique, 109

U

uncertainty, 3, 6, 10, 14, 16, 18, 20–21, 24,
    33, 56, 64, 67, 116, 122, 124
  career, 23
  navigate, 21
  reducing, 20
uncomfortable situation, 32

unconscious competence, 85, 100, 125
unconscious feelings, 98
unconscious incompetence, 82
uneasiness, 14–15, 87
unhappiness, 104
unintended consequences, 8
unordered domain, 17
unpredictability, 17, 19

V

value, 5, 12–13, 25, 43, 45, 64–66, 82–83,
    89, 91–92
vulnerability, 15, 24–25, 62

W

warm-up work, 43
warrior supporter, 77
water regulation, 108
weakness, 25, 74, 96, 113
weight, 23–24, 33, 45, 115, 122
  gaining, 4, 6, 22
  losing, 6
weight-loss process, 23
wholeheartedness, 24
wisdom, 62, 69, 108
  internal, 106, 124
work endeavours, 122
workplace, 46, 59, 71, 78
  anxiety in the, 78
work relationships, 27
workshops, 1, 14, 43–44, 53, 63, 120
work situation, 33
worry, 13–15, 19, 62, 87, 101, 104, 106
  constant, 71
  constant state of, 105–106
worthiness, 24–25
wounds, 46, 124
  old, 111

[Created with **TExtract** / www.Texyz.com]

Related books from KR Publishing

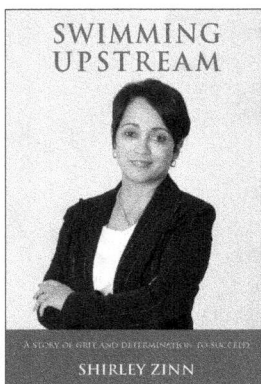

SWIMMING UPSTREAM

A STORY OF GRIT AND DETERMINATION TO SUCCEED

SHIRLEY ZINN

Shirley Zinn's story is one of determination, courage, and triumph over incredible adversity. Her story has lessons for us all. Shirley's story will inspire you and show you that it is possible to achieve your goals, if you are prepared to swim upstream and be single-minded in getting where you want to be.

ISBN: 978-1-86922-589-6
ISBN: 978-1-86922-590-2 (PDF eBook)

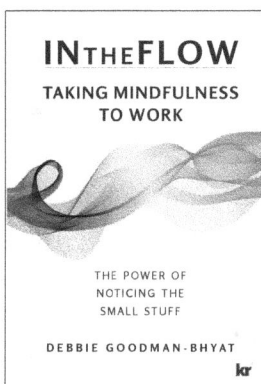

INtheFLOW

TAKING MINDFULNESS TO WORK

THE POWER OF NOTICING THE SMALL STUFF

DEBBIE GOODMAN-BHYAT

kr

This is an uplifting, eloquent and enlightening book that provokes us to wake up and notice the small stuff so that we live more fulfilling lives. The book is packed with enthusiasm about how we can change our lives for the better by providing us with tools, tips and practices that can impact our personal and professional lives.

ISBN: 978-1-86922-632-9
ISBN: 978-1-86922-633-6 (PDF eBook)

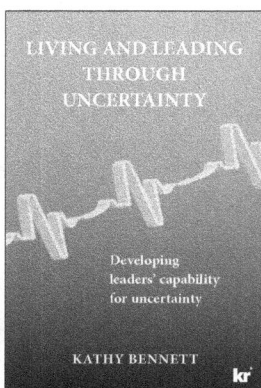

LIVING AND LEADING THROUGH UNCERTAINTY

Developing leaders' capability for uncertainty

KATHY BENNETT

kr

"Uncertainty is opportunity." The author provides an in-depth analysis of uncertainty coupled with self-reflective exercises to help leaders cope in a VUCA world. By weaving together practical techniques for enhancing leadership capability, together with inspiring real-life stories of leaders who embraced uncertainty.

ISBN: 978-1-86922-660-2
ISBN: 978-1-86922-661-9 (PDF eBook)

www.ingramcontent.com/pod-product-compliance
Lightning Source LLC
Chambersburg PA
CBHW070922270326
41927CB00011B/2689